ONE STEP FORWARD TWO STEPS BLACK

Navigating Anti-Black Workplace Culture

Dr Marcelle Moncrieffe-Newman
DBA MA BA(Hons) PGDip PGCert FCIPD

Published by

PEACHES PUBLICATIONS

Published in London by Peaches Publications, 2026.
www.peachespublications.co.uk

ISBN: 9781068384431
Paperback Edition

Images courtesy of Broadway Studios.

British Library Cataloguing in Publication Data: A catalogue record for this book is available from the British Library.

Book cover design: Peaches Publications
Editor: Virginia Rounding & Winsome Duncan
Typesetter: Winsome Duncan
Proofreader: Virginia Rounding

CONTENTS

DEDICATION

To my husband Phil, and my children
Jadine and Nahmarnie, this is for you.

To my parents, Theresa and Perry
Moncrieffe – thank you.

Dad, you are missed every day,
but your memory lives on.

FOREWORD

Dr Marcelle Moncrieffe-Newman is not just a researcher she is someone who has spent over 20 years working in Human Resources, right at the coalface of organisational development. She has seen how workplace cultures change, or more often, how they stubbornly refuse to change, across the different organisations she has worked with. What makes her approach powerful is how she combines her PhD research with her own lived experience. Marcelle is a woman of colour in the UK workspace landscape. She has interviewed more than 30 Black professionals who shared their stories of navigating similar harrowing experiences.

As a Black woman myself, someone who has led teams and spent more than 17 years working primarily in the public sector, I feel a deep connection with Marcelle and the experiences outlined in this book. Our individual stories as Black professionals are different, but there are common threads that run through them all. Across various sectors, different professions and different ages, one thing keeps showing up: the anti-Blackness that is built right into the structures, the policies and the distribution of resources.

Here's something we need to be honest about: we did not choose any of this. We didn't ask to be born, and we certainly didn't ask to be Black in a society that treats Blackness as a problem to be solved. However, society has shaped our experiences, whether we like it or not, and all of that follows us into our workplaces and daily lives.

One Step Forward, Two Steps Black: Navigating Anti-Black Workplace Culture is not just another book going over the same old barriers and difficulties that Black people face in the UK. What Marcelle has done is put Black people front and centre. For years, we have been lumped together under that BAME acronym, which meant our specific experiences got mixed up with those of people from Asian backgrounds and other minority groups. While there might be some similarities, there are fundamental differences in how we experience life in the UK, and they get lost when everything's bundled together.

Marcelle understands something important: she focuses specifically on anti-Blackness because we know racism is about power. She shows how anti-Blackness, this particular form of racism aimed at Black people, actually works in practice. How it shows up in workplaces, how it affects us, and how it gets in the way of our progression.

You may wonder if this book will lose you in academic jargon and theoretical concepts. It will not. This is not a research paper – it is written for everyday people. It is for Black people who want to see their experiences validated, who want practical strategies they can use, and who need to know that what they are going through is real. It's also for non-Black people, white managers and white leaders who are thinking, 'I'm sure something's not right in my organisation – how do we fix this?'

Marcelle writes in plain English because she actually lives this reality every day as a Black woman, and she is also someone who shapes workplace culture from the top. She's right there at the helm, helping organisations become fairer and more equitable. You won't get bogged down in complicated theories. The concepts she mentions give you the language to name what you are seeing when you recognise the patterns and experiences in the book.

Let's be honest, the UK isn't like America or anywhere else in Europe. We have a culture about being refined, keeping that stiff upper lip, and not addressing difficult conversations. This means our issues get swept under the carpet, and Black people get left behind.

In the past five years, we've had Black Lives Matter, COVID hitting Black communities harder than anyone else, the Child Q case, footballers getting racially abused after Euro 2020, and then the summer riots in 2024. Yet we still have people saying the UK is not racist. I always wonder: what's going on here? The people who put up those 'No dogs, no Irish, no Blacks' signs are still alive. They've had children. Families shape society, and we know how values get passed down. Yes, we've had laws passed – the Race Relations Act from 1976, and then everything was rolled into the Equality Act 2010. But look at employment tribunals. Every single day, there are hundreds, if not thousands, of workplace discrimination cases being heard in the courts. Black professionals are getting hit with disciplinary actions and performance reviews more than their non-white peers.

Something is definitely going on. The fact that there are so few Black people at the top of British society is shocking. I discussed this in my TEDx talk back in 2023, and nearly three years later, not much has changed.

What's brilliant about this book is that you're going to see the evidence. It's not just stories or opinions – it's right there in the policies, in how organisations work from top to bottom. The private sector, public sector, charities, government, and even your local businesses. It's everywhere. Marcelle shows you all of this in a way that takes you along for the journey. You're never left wondering what she means – if something doesn't click, you can go back and reread it until it makes sense.

What makes this book different is that Marcelle doesn't just list all the problems Black people face at work. She discusses how we cope – the range of strategies we use to get by, to excel, and to navigate our way through these workplaces. She demonstrates how we can fight back against anti-Black attitudes, both individually and collectively.

This book is meant to spark change and offer hope. It is for those organisations, HR people, leaders and CEOs who are thinking, 'I know diversity and inclusion have had their ups and downs, but I genuinely want a fair workplace where everyone gets treated properly and can do their best work. I want to value all my staff equally.' This book gives you the roadmap to speak out against oppression.

It's about solutions and working together. For those who support Afro-Caribbean people, let's figure out together how we can be a beacon of change to one another. It is not about the blame game; it is about how we pick ourselves up and build workplaces where everyone can succeed together.

What I hope happens when you finish reading is that you feel inspired and ready to make changes. Perhaps you cannot transform your entire company overnight, but you can start with your team or department, one step at a time – and perhaps by buying each of them a copy of *One Step Forward, Two Steps Black*!

Ngozi Cadmus
TEDx Speaker, Founder of Happiworkers

ACKNOWLEDGEMENTS

To my husband Phil, without whom none of this would be possible, you are my rock and my life partner. You have been by my side through it all, behind the scenes sharing the load: the late nights, the joy, the sorrow, discussing ideas and making sure I did not give up. You have read numerous drafts, improved my writing and given me many ideas to enrich the quality of the content. What a journey! I love you and I thank you.

To my wonderful parents, Theresa and Perry Moncrieffe, who taught me to reach for the stars and follow my dreams. Thank you for your love, encouragement and support. It's hard to believe that my dad passed away in 2024 and will not get to read this book – so, Perry Lloyd Moncrieffe, I hope you approve.

Nahmarnie, my beautiful daughter, you are a ball of energy and light who kept me motivated throughout this journey. I remember how upset you were when you learned this was not a children's book! Jadine, my beautiful first-born daughter, you have given me encouragement and support along this journey, and I am in awe of the young woman you have become.

Desiree, my inspirational sister, you have been there with me every step of the way. You always let me know that there is nothing I cannot achieve, your unwavering faith and belief in me have been a constant source of strength. 2024 was a tough year, but we got through it, somehow. To my siblings, Stephen, Allen, Gregory and Jennifer – thank you.

To all the anonymous participants, I thank you for your time and your continued support. Some of you have given me additional insights and guidance which I dearly appreciate. We will stand firm in our pursuit of justice and progress; the experiences you have endured have not been in vain.

This book would not have been possible without my PhD research. I would like to thank Professor Nelarine Cornelius for being a dedicated and motivational PhD supervisor over a four-year period. You supported me through life's ups and downs, including the pandemic and the rewrites – thank you. To my PhD examiners, Dr Tom Farrington and Dr Jane Holgate, thank you for an uplifting viva voce experience. Jane, I will never forget you telling me that my work needed to be shared more widely – here it is!

To Winsome Duncan of Peaches Publications, my amazing publisher who helped me to the finishing line when I thought I simply had too much to juggle. To my lovely niece Dejuan, for stepping in and helping your aunty with childcare and teaching me about connecting with the younger generation!

To Miriam Manderson, firstly for the fabulous afrobeats exercise classes, secondly for your incredible book *From Hood to Headship* and lastly for connecting me with publishing companies that allowed me to turn my book into a reality. Your amazing sister Julia has always been a constant source of friendship and support too – just a lovely family.

Professor Dave Phoenix OBE – thank you for providing me with the space to complete my PhD while juggling a demanding role. Professor Deborah Johnston MBE – thank you for offering words of wisdom regarding sharing my PhD more widely. Professor Calvin Morley MBE – for allowing me the honour of introducing your inaugural professorship lecture.

John Barradell OBE – for the conversations, encouragement and wisdom. Jinjer Kandola MBE – for being a true ambassador and role model; thank you for your perceptive contribution to this book. To Peter Cheese – thank you for being interested in this topic and taking the time to share your ideas. Nels Abbey – for your friendship and for not being afraid to speak out. Jo Larbie – for being a brilliant coach and mentor; you got me through some difficult times. Christina Brooks – thank you for believing in me and, of course, for your insightful reflections in this book. Shani Newbold – for championing me.

Cecilia Crossley – for the stimulating conversation and safe space you provide for HR Leaders. Amy Morris – for our brilliant podcast and your belief in me. Maria Gayle, my second mum – I appreciate our regular check-ins and your presence at all the special occasions you kindly make the time to attend.

PREFACE

The title *One Step Forward Two Steps Black* speaks to the painful truth that for Black people, even moments of career progress can be short-lived, overshadowed by setbacks that push them further back than where they began. It reflects the deep frustration of striving, achieving, and believing change is possible, only to have that hope undone by barriers that strip away hard-won employment gains and leave lasting scars. Yet, it also stands as a call to action: reminding us that resilience, solidarity, and courage can transform career experiences into steps toward lasting change.

While studying for my Master's degree, I approached a senior lecturer to enquire about pursuing a doctorate. The response was that she would not endorse me because, in her opinion, I was not 'good enough'. The barefaced cheek of it! This was despite securing top grades in my modules.

My dream of embarking on a PhD did not die, but I put my dreams on hold as I entered the world of work and then subsequently started to raise my family. Ten years later, my desire was still there, and I approached my line manager to request sponsorship to undertake my PhD; this request was denied. A few years later, I approached another line manager and, for the third time, my request was denied.

Having not received support on three occasions, I decided that I needed to approach this differently. My dream was still alive, and it was now 15 years since I had originally asked my university lecturer to support my PhD application. By now I had moved on to a new organisation. I realised that I just needed to start the PhD by myself without seeking permission. I enrolled on a PhD programme and informed my employer that I had done so.

No need to make a request to my line manager, no opportunity for my request to be rejected. And that is how the journey towards achieving my PhD began. Sometimes, you just need to believe in yourself, persevere and do it! But it's a window into the circuitous journey many Black people endure when they attempt to progress, as 15 years was a significant duration to wait.

CHAPTER 1

WHY WE CAN'T JUST 'KEEP CALM AND CARRY ON'

I can be changed by what happens to me,
but I refuse to be reduced by it.

Maya Angelou

Introduction

I sometimes feel as though the more things on the surface appear to change in terms of career progression for Black people in the UK, the more things stay the same. If you are unaware of, or have forgotten what it means or feels like, to be a Black employee in the UK today, this book will serve as a detailed insight into the lived experiences of Black employees, in addition to providing historical contexts that will depict an unchanged path for an ethnic group that has been integral to the UK for centuries.

While writing this book, I was challenged to answer the question: why should White people care about how Black people are treated at work? My answer is this: White people should care about the treatment of Black people in UK workplaces because racial discrimination not only harms individuals but also negatively impacts workplace culture, society and the economy. Research consistently shows that diverse and inclusive workplaces outperform their competitors, with diverse teams being 35% more likely to outperform and 87% better at making decisions (Watch This Space, 2024).

However, the reality for many Black employees in the UK is far from ideal. A staggering 76% of Black, Black British, Caribbean or African respondents report experiencing discrimination at work or during job hunting (CIPDHR, 2025). This chimes with the countless studies that scientifically prove that racism exists in all areas of life (West, 2025).

In the work context, this systemic inequality leads to underutilised talent, reduced innovation and lost economic opportunities. For instance, addressing racial disparities could potentially add £24 billion per year to the UK economy (Business in the Community, 2025). Moreover, workplace discrimination affects employee wellbeing and productivity, with 19% of affected employees reporting negative impacts on their mental health (Black History Month, 2024).

By actively caring about and addressing these issues, White people can contribute to creating a more equitable, productive and prosperous society for all. However, it does seem strange to me that we need to establish the business case for people to be treated in a fair and just manner, but that's just the world we live in and the reason I felt compelled to write this book.

Did you know that one of the most significant issues facing Black employees in the UK today is underrepresentation in leadership positions? According to the Parker Review Report (2024), which focuses on ethnic diversity on UK boards, only 1% of FTSE 100 directors are Black, and in the FTSE 250 less than 2% of director roles are held by Black employees. This lack of representation is not just a problem for Black professionals but is also a challenge for the workplace, our society, and for Black employees' ability to be integral contributors to the UK's future.

Underrepresentation is not the only issue that Black professionals face in the UK workplace; they also face systemic barriers to career progression and advancement. A 2017 study by the Chartered Institute of Personnel and Development (CIPD) found that Black and ethnically diverse employees are significantly less likely to be promoted to management positions than their White counterparts (Chartered Institute of Personnel and Development, 2017). Extensive research has proven that this is due to a combination of factors, including bias, lack of sponsorship, mentorship and allyship, discrimination, microaggression and negative stereotypes. Although the study was carried out eight years ago, little has changed.

A 2020 Business in the Community report found that 51% of ethnically diverse employees have experienced racism in the workplace, and 30% have experienced bullying or harassment; this affected all levels of employee as, of the c. 75,000 respondents (over three combined iterations of the survey), 66% were educated to Master's level and above. These experiences have immeasurable impacts on wellbeing, mental health and career prospects, but little has been done to reverse this trend.

The lack of equity and ethnic representation in leadership positions means that organisations are missing out on valuable perspectives and ideas that would undoubtedly drive innovation and growth. It also means that Black professionals are not being given the same opportunities to succeed and contribute to their full potential.

To address the current state of the Black employee in the UK, there needs to be a collective effort to create more inclusive and equitable workplaces. This requires a willingness to confront uncomfortable truths, address biases that have historically and incorrectly been branded as unconscious, and to create policies and practices that promote practical actions that will ensure sustainable anti-racist workplaces. It requires leaders to take an active role in creating change, and for all employees to be accountable for their actions and behaviours in the workplace.

There are some positive steps being taken to recognise the Black employee experience in the UK. The Black Lives Matter movement protests of 2020 highlighted the need for change and led to many organisations hiring equity and inclusion leads to review their strategies on race. The Parker Review set out voluntary targets for greater ethnic diversity on UK boards. While these steps were just the beginning, recent events (see chapter 2) and a leap to the right wing of political discourse have led to a backlash against equity and inclusion. More on this later. For now, I want to tell you a bit about my background.

A Love Story

In the early 1960s, as the winds of change swept across the British Empire, two young souls embarked on separate journeys that would intertwine their destinies and shape the course of their lives. Their stories, like countless others, form the rich tapestry of Britain's post-war immigration narrative.

At the tender age of 12, a young girl bade farewell to the lush, sun-drenched shores of Grenada. With a heart full of hope and a suitcase packed with dreams, she boarded 'the Montserrat', a vessel that would carry her across the vast Atlantic. For three long weeks, the ship became her world, a floating microcosm of Caribbean life as it made its way through the azure waters, stopping at Dominica and Tenerife.

The journey was more than a physical passage; it was a transition between worlds, from the familiar warmth of the Caribbean to the unknown shores of Britain. As the Montserrat finally docked in Southampton, the girl stepped on to English soil, her young mind barely grasping the magnitude of the change she was about to experience.

From Southampton, she boarded a train bound for London, her eyes wide with wonder at the unfamiliar landscape rushing past the windows. It was on this very journey, however, that she received her first bitter taste of the prejudice that lurked beneath the surface of her new home. A passenger, seeing her dark skin, hurled a racial slur, likening her to a monkey. The words stung, a harsh welcome to a land that had promised opportunity but delivered a cold reality.

Meanwhile, another story was unfolding. A 17-year-old boy from Jamaica turned down a career as a trainee mechanic, deciding instead to take the option his mother had given him for a better opportunity. So he took to the skies, leaving behind the Caribbean heat for the grey skies of England. His journey, though shorter in duration, was no less significant. The airplane carried him across the same ocean his future wife had traversed by ship, though neither yet knew of the other's existence.

The girl found herself in Northwest London, reunited with her parents who had paved the way before her. The boy settled in West London, surrounded by relatives who had already established a foothold in this foreign land. Both faced the challenges of adapting to a new culture, a new climate, and a society that was not always welcoming.

As they grew into adulthood, their paths would cross, their shared experiences of migration forming a bond that would blossom into love. Their stories, beginning with these journeys, would become part of a larger narrative – the story of the Windrush generation and their descendants, who would go on to shape modern Britain in countless ways, enriching its culture, challenging its prejudices and redefining what it meant to be British. I am proud to say that this young couple were my parents.

Growing Up

I was the second youngest of my five siblings and financial constraints resulted in my childhood being difficult at times. Having been an agricultural worker in Jamaica, my father's first role in the UK was as a porter at Hammersmith Hospital, first in the laundry department, and then in the canteen. Being new to the UK, my dad had to quickly learn what a 'spag bol' was in order to send out the correct meals from the hospital kitchen ('spag bol' is the slang name for spaghetti bolognese for the uninitiated!).

My dad then worked in a series of factories, including McVitie's in Park Royal, West London, where many Caribbean arrivals worked in the 1960s. I remember the period as a child when we grew up on a staple diet of broken biscuits, the perk of my dad working for a biscuit manufacturer!

Following a period as a mini-cab driver, my dad pursued training as an electrician with the intention of establishing his own business. Prior to this, he had prioritised providing for his family over furthering his education. However, his business plans were unfortunately derailed when his business partner was discovered to be a fraudster. As a result, he redirected his career path and managed a Youth Centre for a time before transitioning into a role as a bus driver, a position he would hold for the remainder of his career.

My mum had aspirations of being a doctor but was told by her headteacher that this would be impossible to achieve. After finishing secondary school in the UK, to make ends meet, my mum worked in a couple of factory jobs, first making powder compacts and then making spindles. Mum then worked in Woolworths in Harlesden, Northwest London, as a sales advisor in the toy section; it is now a 'One Pound store'. Later on, my mum started working as a cashier for Harrods. It was during this period that my parents met.

My dad's version of events is that they (my parents) met on the bus and my dad had to pay my mum's bus fare because she did not have enough money; however, my mum vehemently disputes this. My mum's version is that she was on the bus and on her way to pay 'partner' money for her mum and so did not have any small notes or coins. 'Partner' in this context is a savings plan used by the Caribbean community when they first arrived in the UK as it was very difficult for them to secure loans from the high street banks. It became a long-standing source of family entertainment for each of my parents to recount their very different versions of what happened on that 260 bus in 1967!

Although Harrods is a prestigious retailer, my mum was earning a grand total of £12 per week! Mum recalls asking for a pay rise at Harrods in the late 1960s, which took her salary to £24 a week. It sounds like such a low wage today, but the pay rise, along with my dad's income, enabled my parents to buy their first home in Wembley where they would remain for the duration of their marriage of over 50 years until my dad sadly succumbed to cancer.

My mum took a career break to raise her children and then had a long social work career for the London Borough of Brent.

As well as being a long-standing magistrate, my mum was a founding member of the Caribbean Social Club and latterly the WISE (West Indian Self Effort) Project which ran Saturday schools and community groups for the Black community in Northwest London to supplement mainstream services. Whilst we lived in meagre surroundings with limited resources throughout my childhood, the lack of material wealth was more than compensated for by love and togetherness.

My primary and secondary school years are littered with despondent memories due to my severe eczema and lack of encouragement from teachers. (Eczema, also known as atopic dermatitis, is a chronic inflammatory skin condition that causes redness, itching and irritation. It is a common condition that can affect people of all ages, but it typically begins in childhood. The exact cause of eczema is not fully understood, but it is believed to result from a combination of genetic, environmental and immune system factors.)

In my case, I had very visible childhood eczema which made me a target for playground bullying. I attended a state comprehensive school in the Northwest London Borough of Brent in the 1990s – it was tough.

Academically, teachers constantly reminded me of their low expectations of me in relation to a promising career of any kind, and socially I spent my time trying to avoid bullies. Luckily, I have an older sister – her name is Desiree. At school, Desiree was not only fierce, but she was popular, trendy and my biggest advocate. Nobody dared to mess with me when Desiree was around. It was just such a shame she had to leave two years before me!

There was a diverse mix of students from a wide catchment area at school. A Black cohort from Northwest London, South Asians from North Brent and Harrow, a White contingent from the surrounding area, and also an influx of refugees from East Africa – altogether a huge multicultural mix.

Despite the lack of many privileges that were afforded to my White fellow students, despite the lack of faith shown in me, despite the absence of allyship, mentorship and sponsorship, despite facing discrimination and a plethora of obstacles, my parents' desire for me to be successful and benefit from their hard work has been the primary reason that I have been driven to make a difference.

After finishing school, I worked in several part-time jobs for companies such as BT and British Airways to help fund my higher education. When I completed a Bachelor's degree in law, it fuelled my interest in employment law, which in turn steered me towards completing a Master's degree in Human Resource Management.

Seeing the desire in me, my family assisted with a successful application to the government of Grenada for a three-month internship with their Human Resources department. This ultimately helped convince me to pursue my interest in the people side of workplace culture and consequently led me to choose a career in Human Resources (HR) over one in law.

Early Career Experiences

Despite forging a successful executive career in the field of Human Resources, intersectionality – i.e. the interconnected nature of being both a woman and a Black person – has made my career journey both complicated and challenging.

Finding my first job in HR was tough, and I found myself in a classic catch-22 situation of being a graduate with two degrees and a professional qualification, but little work experience and few opportunities to secure such experience. Despite this challenge, I eventually landed an HR role and started gaining hands-on professional graduate-level experience. However, right from the start of my career, I faced discrimination that I needed to navigate.

In my first graduate HR job, a senior manager requested that I take on significant additional responsibilities for no extra pay; when I raised this disparity, my request was rejected. I felt saddened to know that, after all this studying, my initial experience felt like exploitation. I couldn't put my finger on what was happening at first; it was just a question in my mind about why I was being treated this way. However, I felt disheartened at these initial frosty interactions. I quickly learned that I needed to advocate for myself, but found that there were consequences for doing so. Navigating the world of work was hard enough without having to factor in discrimination and bias.

In time, I secured a role elsewhere where I felt the remuneration was more commensurate with the role. When I handed in my resignation, a senior manager covertly ordered an IT technician to download all my files from my desktop. On discovering this, I confronted the senior manager, who did not deny it and proceeded to tell me that he was worried I would tamper with data before I left. I felt very hurt to know that I was not trusted because I had resigned. I also felt very angry and betrayed. This reconfirmed that I had made the right decision to leave that organisation.

In another early HR role, I worked in a team where every team member had the same job. One of my White colleagues was always complaining about money and the costs of working in central London. However, one day I noticed that he had stopped complaining, was buying expensive coffees every morning and was suddenly very positive about his job. At this point I discovered that he had been awarded a pay rise. When I queried it with my line manager, I was told my White colleague was given the pay rise so that he would not resign for a better job, as I had just done.

How ironic that my colleague had been awarded a pay rise based on my endeavours to secure a new role. I, on the other hand, was never approached to find out if I would have stayed in my role if the same pay rise had been offered to me. At this early stage of my career, I was learning how to navigate being an HR professional whilst being Black. But I was also starting to feel quite low; would this be my employee experience moving forward? Or was the maltreatment unique to those organisations? In other words, were my previous organisations just rotten apples?

As my expertise grew, enabling me to gain several promotions to the position of Head of HR, I noticed a continued pattern of racial discrimination in the form of bullying, harassment and microaggressions. I now started to feel depressed and disillusioned. This was now turning out to be a systemic problem.

Am I the Only One?

Curious and bewildered as to whether these challenges were unique to me, I became aware that other Black and ethnically diverse employees were having similar experiences, and I soon realised that I was not alone. I witnessed a senior Black professional hounded out of her role through institutional bullying and harassment, leaving her broken and needing to take significant time out of her chosen profession.

Another senior Black colleague was bullied and racially harassed and forced to leave her role and successfully won an employment tribunal. In other cases, senior Black professionals were persistently being discriminated against and bullied out of their jobs. To provide context, bullying someone out of their role is achieved through a persistent combination of microaggressions, systemic biases, harassment and the setting of unrealistic objectives with little or no resources to achieve them, so that in turn, the individual can be branded as incompetent or suffer a severe lack of confidence in their own abilities.

I set about improving my network with other Black and ethnically diverse employees to understand their experiences and observations. In time, Black and ethnically diverse staff disclosed that they were being unfairly blocked from promotion or receiving unwarranted negative and biased performance reviews. I began to see a trend!

As my career progressed, I continued to experience workplace racism. For example, one of my direct reports constantly left a pencil with a golliwog[1] head on my allocated shelf. I felt offended, sickened and shocked. Strangely, though, I also felt embarrassed.

When I raised this with my line manager, a White man, he said to me, 'Marcelle, don't you think this is racial discrimination?' Of course, it was racial discrimination, but it was somehow difficult for me to say it out loud at work. Isn't that strange? But that's how racism works. I somehow felt that, if I admitted that it was racist, it would make people question

[1] A golliwog is a racist caricature of Black people.

whether I should be in my role. In other words, I was blaming myself rather than my racist colleague.

When the racist colleague was confronted about her behaviour, I recall her saying that she could not be racist because she had a Black friend. I thought to myself, oh please, not that old line! And the fact that she said it to me in person with a straight face was the icing on the cake. In another role, I was demoted while on maternity leave. I later discovered the company planned to replace me with the White person covering my maternity leave. To me, these actions were racist, sexist and illegal. I was appalled and very anxious, given that I had just had a baby. This should have been a time of joy but instead I was depressed and isolated.

A few years later, I applied for a role in a public sector organisation. However, racial profiling led to me being told that I would not fit in with White 'intellectual' senior leaders there, a biased subjective judgement that showed total disregard for my academic and professional achievements to date. I felt upset that I was being underestimated in such an obvious way. I came to the realisation that it was common to experience intersectional discrimination due to race and gender, and I began to comprehend that these instances of discrimination would become more frequent and intense as I sought to fulfil my career aspirations.

Unfortunately, it is a common phenomenon that Black people speaking out against racial discrimination is a precursor to an acrimonious exit from the organisation, or at best a stagnated career, and due to a disparity in the number of Black peers, it can be difficult to find a trusted confidant to turn to for help or to seek counsel internally.

When I spoke with Black colleagues, they agreed that addressing workplace discrimination or disadvantage required caution, as it could lead to abrupt dismissal.

What Can I Do?

With an overarching desire to learn from and share workplace experiences, I decided to act and began working on a part-time postgraduate course to become a doctoral researcher. My goal was to understand more about how workplace culture affects the career progression of Black employees. Having successfully completed the doctoral research course, I then commenced a part-time doctorate.

For my doctoral research titled *What impact does the workplace culture of public sector institutions have on the career progression of Black employees?* I talked to hundreds of Black professionals and formally interviewed 30. I used the constructivist grounded theory research method, looking at the issue through the lens of critical race theory. It took a lot of work to balance studying part-time for a doctorate with working full-time in a senior demanding job and raising a family. As I often say, the struggle is real people!

Talking to Black and ethnically diverse people about their experiences was cathartic and relatable and enabled them to feel heard. I felt honoured to hear the accounts, as many of the contributors were sharing their experiences for the first time.

Finishing the doctorate was a challenging endeavour, to say the least! I faced many obstacles, such as unsupportive employers and time constraints, but I compensated for this with my motivation and drive to complete the research. During the COVID-19 pandemic lockdowns, I finished my write-up. When I successfully defended my thesis, the examiners praised my research as groundbreaking and encouraged me to publish my findings – and I am now ready to share this with you.

Motivated by a profound desire to illuminate the experiences of Black professionals in the UK workplace, I felt compelled to write this book. By sharing my personal journey alongside the in-depth accounts of Black professionals I interviewed, I aim to shed light on the challenges and obstacles that Black employees face in their careers.

My hope is that Black employees who relate to these experiences will find solace in knowing they are not alone in how they feel, how they have been treated, and how they can navigate these situations. For advocates, allies and those with privilege who possess a genuine desire to create and maintain equitable workplaces, I offer lived experiences and actionable recommendations to inspire meaningful change.

Workplace Cultures Must Transform

This book aspires to ignite a dialogue about the current state of Black representation in the UK workplace while catalysing action. Such actions may include speaking out against racism and discrimination, supporting organisations and initiatives that champion equity and inclusion, and leveraging privilege to advocate for the advancement of others.

For those who have not personally encountered discrimination or microaggressions, I aim to provide insights and understanding to help improve organisational culture and the employee experience for all. By recounting the lived experiences of Black professionals, I hope to nurture empathy and compassion for those grappling with systemic barriers to career development and advancement.

I want to encourage leaders to critically examine their policies and practices in relation to racial inclusion. Additionally, I seek to motivate individuals to reflect on their own biases and behaviours while taking actionable steps toward creating balanced and fair work environments.

I also wish to equip young Black professionals with the knowledge and preparation needed to navigate the workplace confidently, avoiding common pitfalls and striving for enriching and positive career experiences. For future leaders, I hope this book serves as a guide to embracing ethical and inclusive leadership behaviours.

Ultimately, my aim is to contribute to the creation of a more inclusive and diverse society, where every employee, regardless of ethnicity, has the opportunity to thrive and realise their full potential. It is my deepest desire that these words inspire readers to act, collaborate and advocate for a better and more equitable world for all.

We are about to go on a journey together and I want you to have your thinking cap firmly on, I have created space for you to reflect at the end of the book, so please feel free to visit the notes section at key points so you can capture your thoughts and importantly your points of action as you read the book.

> *By championing the case for increased senior racially diverse representation and inclusivity in the workplace, we can build a brighter future for ourselves and upcoming generations.*
>
> Dr Marcelle Moncrieffe-Newman

Overview

I intend to highlight the impact of workplace culture on the career progression of Black employees in public sector organisations in the UK and further shine a light on the underrepresentation of Black people in leadership positions across all industries. It is essential to understand this because, despite what some people might think, racism and bias are still major career barriers in Britain, and the disparity in the number of Black leaders in organisations has a knock-on effect on junior and middle managers who lack role models, advocacy and allyship from people who look like them.

We will examine the lived experiences of Black and ethnically diverse employees and reference decades of research to help us understand the factors that contribute to diverse representation and discrimination, and introduce suggestions for policies and practices that can help improve underrepresentation in organisations.

Some organisations in the UK have made progress in improving racial diversity at senior levels, but this progress is experienced at a glacial pace or not felt at all by Black and ethnically diverse employees. Even though some employers claim to be equal-opportunity employers, there has been little change in the representation of Black and ethnically diverse employees over the past decade across all industries.

Further, many of those who have achieved success will have done so through their own personal efforts rather than through organisational support. To help provide context to the notions that will be introduced, the voices of Black professionals will be foregrounded to better understand their perspectives on career progression in UK workplaces.

The Race at Work Charter: One Year On (2019) report from Business in the Community presents the findings of 108 employers who disclosed their organisations' current progress against the five Race Charter principles. The report found that many employers lack goals to increase racial diversity at board and executive levels. Many have gaping ethnicity pay gaps, have never investigated racial harassment and bullying, and do not have diversity performance goals for their managers.

These findings show that addressing workplace racial discrimination, bias and inequality has not been deemed a priority for corporate leadership and HR teams, and some of those that do have quotas and targets have set them well below current national ethnicity demographic figures, meaning that their workforces or senior leadership targets will never be likely to be representative of the communities they serve.

As you read these pages, you will gain a deeper understanding of the challenges that Black professionals face in the workplace. It is not enough to simply engage with this material and walk away. You are invited to take bold and uncomfortable actions to drive change.

The accounts of discrimination, microaggressions and underrepresentation that you will encounter in this book are not fictional, theoretical or abstract concepts. They are real, lived experiences that are happening right now in workplaces across the UK. Black professionals are being deprived of advancement, underrated and experiencing the harsh end of racial discrimination through the systemic barriers placed in front of them. This is not just a problem for Black professionals, but a problem for us all. It is an issue for the workplace, for our society, and for the future of our children and generations to come.

Overall, even though Black professionals can be extremely resilient, you will find that the treatment of Black employees in the UK really does take the biscuit. However, through writing this book and awakening progressive employers, I aim to ensure that the poor experiences of Black employees will not always be 'just the way the cookie crumbles' and that a more prosperous alternative awaits.

Critical Race Theory

It is theorised that racial bias is inherent in many parts of Western society, especially in its legal and social institutions, based on them being primarily designed for and implemented by White people – collectively, these notions are known as critical race theory (CRT) (Delgado & Stefancic, 2017).

CRT recognises that legal, political and social systems are historical and continue to be used to reinforce and create racial inequalities (Delgado & Stefancic, 2017). It also acknowledges the historical and lived experiences of marginalised groups – in this case, Black people in the UK – and how these experiences shape their current reality.

CRT provides a useful framework for understanding the ways in which bias and structural racism operate in society, including the UK. The development of CRT in the 1970s highlighted the need for new strategies and theories to address the subtler forms of racial discrimination, such as microaggressions and micro-incivilities, that were becoming increasingly prevalent (Delgado & Stefancic, 2017).

The themes of CRT are central to understanding the experiences of Black people in the UK and the ways in which racism operates in society and the workplace. CRT asserts that racism is an ordinary and normalised experience for Black people and that colour-blind approaches can only address the most obvious forms of discrimination. The theory also asserts that all White people benefit from racism, regardless of their socio-economic status, and that race is a social construct rather than a biological or scientific one (Delgado & Stefancic, 2017).

Intersectionality (Crenshaw, 1989) and the unique voices of Black people are also acknowledged in CRT, and storytelling and recounting experiences are encouraged to bring attention to the effects of oppression. These themes are relevant to understanding the experiences of Black people in UK workplaces and will help to make sense of career progression challenges and workplace culture.

The definition highlights the difficulties caused by dominant groups altering historical events and legacies that affect people of colour. Some literature argues that there is a drive to erase the memories of discrimination and oppression and remove them from historical records. It is crucial to keep this context in mind and grasp its significance, as it serves as an important reference for comprehending current discrimination faced by Black people and finding ways to bring about change.

CRT has faced criticism for suggesting that only ethnically diverse scholars have the ability to address racial issues. Attempts have also been made by right-wing commentators, white supremacists, politicians and scholars to discredit CRT in its entirety. This attempt stems from the incendiary and false notion that racism does not exist and therefore CRT cannot be required to explain a non-existent phenomenon. This is such a bizarre notion to me but, yes, there are very loud prominent voices that will tell you that racism does not exist. It is all in our heads. Only, it does exist, and the very people who wish to silence Black people are the main proponents of it.

I've been reading books that extol the virtues of manifestation – apparently, all I need to do is think of the life I want, place it on a vision board and it will come true. Well, I for one would love to manifest a world free of racism. I'll let you know how that goes! But returning to those who tell us racism does not exist: do they think we want to spend our time dealing with racism? No, we don't.

We too would love to live normal lives. If we had the choice, we would not be spending time on the topic of racism. In time, maybe there will be a study that looks at the amount of wasted time Black people have to spend dealing with racism over the course of their lifetime. I for one would like my time and the money associated with that lost time back. Can I have a refund, please?

Further, there has been internal debate among CRT scholars regarding the focus on perceived middle-class racial concerns, such as microaggressions, racial slurs, unconscious bias and positive action. I argue that these issues are not exclusive to the middle class, but rather, they are part of the evolving nature of racism. This is the type of racism that people think they can get away with because it often flies under the radar of weak racial discrimination legislation and even weaker organisational policies. Remember the 'I have a Black friend' comment I was subjected to when I called out a racist colleague? People are able to hide behind the 'I didn't mean it like that' pretext.

From a CRT perspective, racism is considered to be widespread, systematic and deeply ingrained in society. This framework can be applied to cultural and racial experiences in the

UK. Black people in both the USA and the UK have a shared history of racism and discrimination.

One of the main differences between African Americans and Black Britons is that for African Americans the British slave ships took Africans directly to America in chains, whereas for Black Britons, the British slave ships took them to the Caribbean and many then travelled to the UK, based on promises of contributing to a society that would never truly accept them. Racial equality has advanced slowly in both countries, which for me made CRT a suitable lens to use in my UK-based research. More on this later. While my dad travelled to the UK from Jamaica, one of his brothers, my uncle Harold, went to the USA, as did several other family members. Therefore, I have ties to both the USA and the UK.

Back to Black – the Root of the Problem

I think it is important to use a historical lens to reveal what has gone before as it offers richer insights into the experiences and political landscape relating to Black people. I always have a desire to understand, as a race of people – how did we get here? I ask the questions: Why are things the way they are? Will our position as Black people in the UK ever improve? What keeps holding us back? These questions always lead me to wanting to examine what has gone before and to understand our history.

Using this conceptual frame, we can ask the question, why does senior-level representation of Black people in the workplace remain so low? Even in sport – for example, in the football premiership where 43% of players are Black, only 1% fill coaching positions and none are managers (Sky Sports, 2024).

Further, a CRT perspective would argue that revisionist history is required to evidence the often-suppressed lived experience of Black people. It may surprise people to know that Black people have been in the UK since AD 3 when legions of African soldiers came as part of the Roman conquest (Black Presence in Britain, 2010). In the seventeenth and eighteenth centuries, many Black people were also brought over to the UK forcibly as domestic slaves (Fryer, 1984). They served wealthy households and merchants, either in the UK or connected to the Caribbean or North America.

The eighteenth century was a time of the British slave trade (Chater, 2010:3), but some Black people also came freely and stayed (Fryer, 1984). In 1760, it is estimated that there were approximately 20,000 Black people living in the UK (Fryer, 1984).

This points to the many types of Black migration to the UK, yet despite their long history with Britain, Black people still face challenges in achieving social justice and equality, reflecting historical power dynamics. This history demonstrates that the relationship between Black people and the UK has always been an unequal one, with Black people largely deemed uncivilised and subordinate to White people, and these beliefs impact on their treatment in the UK today.

The British Empire profited immensely from the transatlantic slave trade, as it facilitated the economic growth and expansion of Britain's colonies in the Americas and the Caribbean. The forced labour of enslaved Africans contributed to the development of large-scale plantations, which produced valuable cash crops such as sugar, tobacco and cotton.

The Western world valued these commodities highly, and their exportation allowed Britain to amass great wealth, strengthen its global influence and become the empire that it has been universally recognised as being.

It is essential to acknowledge that the repercussions of this dark chapter in history have persisted for generations. Recognising the long-lasting effects of institutional racism, calls for reparations have grown louder in recent years. Earlier, I mentioned wanting a refund for racism – well, the idea of reparations centres on compensating descendants of enslaved people for the multi-generational suffering and disadvantage caused by the slave trade and colonialism.

Commonwealth leaders and former British colonies are increasingly calling for the UK to provide reparations for its role in the transatlantic slave trade and colonialism. This issue has gained momentum in recent years, with growing pressure for reparations from Commonwealth heads of government (BBC News, 2024a). Despite the UK government's insistence that reparations are not on the official agenda, diplomatic sources indicate that discussions are underway to facilitate further research and initiate a 'meaningful dialogue' on the issue. A 2023 report co-authored by a UN judge concluded that the UK owes over £18 trillion to 14 Caribbean nations (Bazelon et al., 2023).

Proponents argue that slavery facilitated the rise of Britain as a global player, with its effects filtering down through generations. They point to the £20 million (equivalent to £16–17 billion today) paid to British slave owners as compensation in 1834, while freed slaves received nothing (Bank of England, 2022). These facts clearly demonstrate injustice, and more salt was rubbed into the wound when it was reported that the UK only finished paying off debts to slave-owning families in 2015 (Brown, 2020). Let that sink in. The UK only finished paying the descendants of White slave owners in 2015. That is ridiculous, and yet here Black people are, still dealing with the legacy of slavery through the racism that is rife on a day-to-day basis.

Supporters contend that the legacy of slavery and colonialism continues to affect former colonies through intergenerational trauma, inequities in social indicators, high incarceration rates and endemic poverty (The Week, 2023). Proposed reparations could take various forms, including financial compensation, debt relief for developing nations, investment in infrastructure, education, health and transportation, formal apologies and acknowledgement of historical wrongs. As the debate continues, the issue of reparations remains contentious, with growing pressure from Commonwealth nations and resistance from the UK government (BBC News, 2024b). In addition, museums all over Europe still contain artefacts stolen from African countries – so, in addition to reparations, will these ever be returned?

In the context of the UK workplace, the legacy of slavery and the British Empire's role in perpetuating racial inequality cannot be ignored. Despite the passage of time and the enactment of anti-discrimination legislation, the impact of historical racism lingers in more subtle forms of barriers that hinder the career progression and workplace experiences of Black professionals. A plethora of studies show that Black individuals in the UK face significant disparities in pay, representation in leadership positions, and access to opportunities compared to their White counterparts (Moncrieffe, 2021; Ray, 2019; Ozturk & Berber, 2021).

Whilst racism and the unequal treatment of ethnically diverse people have been features of UK society for hundreds of years, it was only in the 1940s that sociologists (Rush, 2007) started to examine the integration of Black people in Britain. Further studies of Black people in Britain in the 1960s established the start of the UK race relations field.

Sadly, prior to the 1970s, Black people in Britain were not seen as a significant aspect of society. This history is noteworthy as, until the 1970s, there was limited documentation on the integration of Black communities in the UK. This lack of attention to Black people is a factor in the current treatment they receive in the UK today.

Black people from the Commonwealth, including West Africa and the Caribbean, supported the British Army during World War II by working in munitions factories and in many cases they fought on the front lines as infantry soldiers and as pilots. Then in the 1940s and 1950s, due to a labour shortage, the UK government also invited people from the Black Commonwealth to fill low-paying manual and menial jobs (Williams, 2015).

Many of the people who arrived were over-skilled for these roles but made the trip in the hope of a better standard of living and due to a connection with the 'motherland'. The arrival of about 1,000 people from the Caribbean on HMT *Empire Windrush* in 1948, and London Transport hiring employees directly in Barbados in the 1950s, saw a significant increase of people of colour from the Commonwealth in Britain (Sivanandan, 1982). However, this narrative is often misrepresented as Black people arriving to exploit UK resources, when they were actively recruited and actually invited to fill the labour shortage.

Adopting a new identity, the Black migrants in post-war UK identified as Black British yet were seen by White Britons as foreigners due to their skin colour. Early sociologists also held this view, seeing Caribbean migrants as 'dark strangers' (Gilroy & Wilmore, 2021:12). This highlights the contrast of Caribbean people being invited to the UK for their labour and skills, but not being fully accepted due to racial discrimination. This juxtaposition is related to a feeling of not belonging in a country that, for many Black people like me, is the country of their birth.

Caribbean migrants faced prejudice and there were calls to limit immigration. Nevertheless, immigration to the UK continued from West Africa in the 1980s and from East Africa in the 1970s and 90s (Williams, 2015). Unfortunately, work opportunities for Caribbean and African migrants continued to be mostly limited to unskilled or semi-skilled manual labour until the 1970s, and this legacy proved hard to shift even after the 1970s. Not being able to achieve their full potential during this era has continued to impact the subsequent generations of Black people.

The concentration of Caribbean and African communities in cities also created a sense of otherness and exclusion from mainstream society. The result is a legacy of systemic racism and discrimination that continues to affect Black communities in the UK today.

It is important to highlight the historic role of trade unions and activism in advocating for fair treatment and equality for Black workers in the UK. Despite facing discrimination and marginalisation, Black workers continued to organise and fight for their rights, highlighting their resilience and determination to achieve equality and justice in the workplace (Millington, 2011). These efforts have helped to shape the modern UK workplace, where overt discrimination happens less and is now more frequently hidden behind biased actions, exclusion, bullying and harassment, microaggressions and micro-incivilities. However, much more progress is needed to completely eradicate racism.

Despite anti-discrimination legislation being enacted, the exclusion and marginalisation of Black Britons remain a legacy that still affects their opportunities and experiences in society today. The concept of White privilege and the need to address it are crucial in moving towards a more equitable society. The intersection of race with other factors, such as class, unemployment and gender, further exacerbates the disadvantages faced by Black populations.

Previous political discourse and academic research have often grouped all non-White people into the category of Black Asian and minority ethnic – BAME. This has led to a generalisation of the experiences and challenges faced by different ethnicities under the banner of 'BAME', and has contributed to the ongoing failure to recognise the specific and distinct issues faced by each community. For example, Black people tend to face harsher racial discrimination in the UK on a number of fronts, including policing, health, education, immigration and employment. Throughout this book, the terms people of colour, ethnically diverse, and global majority are used to describe individuals and communities whose backgrounds are not considered 'white'.

The notion of Black people being seen as uncivilised and subordinate to White people perpetuates the existing power dynamics, discrimination and racism. It has also been further evidenced by organisations who have conducted an ethnicity pay gap audit, where findings have disclosed the fact that there is a wider gap in relation to the pay of Black people than any other group.

Despite being sought after for their hard work, Black people were frequently the targets of racism and discrimination whilst at work. New migrants from the Commonwealth accepted lower-status jobs than they were qualified for in their home countries, unaware of trade unions and employment law (Sivanandan, 1982). Later, many Black and Asian workers joined unions, particularly in the public sector. However, there were also several strikes by people of colour through the 1960s and 1970s that were not supported by the trade union movement and received little coverage by the UK media (Millington, 2011).

This reference point illuminates that Black and ethnically diverse employees have historically been singled out for worse terms, conditions and treatment, thus highlighting the historically exploitative nature of Black and ethnically diverse labour in the UK.

De-industrialisation occurred in the 1970s, with the result that many unskilled populations became unemployed – a disadvantage which was accompanied by racism in the employment market (Fryer, 1984). Ethnically diverse people were largely seen as disposable labour, as a consequence.

Caribbean and African workers were the first to be laid off if there was not enough work; this led to racial tensions and more concentrated policing. A flashpoint of this was seen in the 1981 Brixton riots which resulted in an official inquiry led by Lord Scarman. Violence in the capital city of the UK was a wake-up call for politicians (Millington, 2011).

During the 1960s, as the American civil rights movement gained momentum, several Black British figures were instrumental in changing race relations in the UK. Paul Stephenson, a youth worker in Bristol, led the successful Bristol Bus Boycott in 1963, which challenged the racist employment practices of the Bristol Omnibus Company (Blackhistorymonth.org.uk, 2021).

Claudia Jones, a Trinidadian-born activist, founded Britain's first major Black newspaper, the *West Indian Gazette*, in 1958 and played a crucial role in organising the first London

Carnival (Jones, 2006). In the late 1960s, the British Black Panthers, including key figures like Altheia Jones-LeCointe and Darcus Howe, emerged to confront racial inequality head-on, fostering a sense of community and identity that would inspire generations to come.

These activists, among others, were pivotal in challenging systemic racism and pushing for legislative changes, mirroring the efforts of their American counterparts during this tumultuous era.

The Bristol Bus Boycott paved the way for the Race Relations Act of 1965, which was enacted to address racial discrimination in public places. It was replaced by the Race Relations Act of 1976 which extended the remit to cover employment and housing and created the Commission for Racial Equality. This legislation was subsequently subsumed into the Equality Act (2010), which covers a range of protected characteristics, including race.

This problematic co-location of race with eight other protected characteristics means racial discrimination is somewhat lost in the legislation. Abbas (2020:18) asserts that the legacy of Black Britons is symbolised by 'their exclusion from structural advantages' and not being treated as full citizens, and that Whiteness 'needs to embrace a politics of discomfort to unsettle the seat of white privilege'. This proposition is supported by a proportion of the literature, which demonstrates that it is inconsequential for organisations to take little or no action to address discrimination and bias.

The official recognition of institutional racism in the Macpherson report, following the racist murder of Stephen Lawrence in 1993 (Macpherson, 1999; Yuval-Davis, 1999; Foster et al., 2005; Millington, 2011) signalled a landmark change in defining deep-seated racism at the heart of historical British institutions, despite the report having been published post hoc, thus exacerbating the reactionary nature of race relations in the UK.

This section looked at the historical context of Black people in the UK to provide a narrative of the societal response to their arrival, prejudicial treatment and other experiences that have shaped the current position. The evolution of equalities legislation has also been discussed. The next section will examine the immigration and integration landscape.

Immigration and Integration

Immigration and integration literature demonstrates that widespread discrimination in the labour market shapes the pattern of access and exclusion (Platt & Nandi, 2020). Li and Heath (2020) found that ethnically diverse people in the UK experience ethnic penalties and unemployment scarring, which places them at higher risk of job loss. Differences in the employment of non-White groups are substantial and nuanced; however, there is a lack of successful policy action to address ethnic inequalities (Byrne et al., 2020).

This picture continues to build the narrative of indifference to tackling inequalities that blights the lives of Black and ethnically diverse people. This speaks to the notion that, if the issues do not impact White people, there is little interest in tackling them. As such, the literature thus far has demonstrated that action to address racial inequality has only been taken as a last resort because of a flashpoint, outpouring or protest.

On 23 June 2016, the UK held a referendum which led to the decision to exit the European Union. The Brexit referendum culminated in 'multiple racisms' being 'evoked by the Leave campaign to secure Britain's exit from the European

Union', including racialised 'nationalism of a "White England" whose state and resources were threatened by white Eastern and Central Europeans and Black and Brown migrants' (Narayan, 2019:959).

These notions are not new but demonstrate the tensions underlying the integration, or lack thereof, of non-White citizens who are viewed as outsiders who exploit welfare and housing and generally take more than they give (Narayan, 2019). This racialised political fearmongering is frequently used to stoke anxieties in the majority population and proves to be a reliable vote winner every time (Narayan, 2019). To draw on these tensions, a significant proportion of Vote Leave campaigners signalled that the referendum was about controlling immigration.

Former UK Independence Party leader, now Reform UK leader and MP Nigel Farage stated that 'mass immigration is still hopelessly out of control and set to get worse if we remain inside the EU' (BBC News, 2016). Comparable assertions were made by Vote Leave campaigner Gisela Stuart who stated that 'voting to remain meant that there would be "no control" over migration from the EU, no matter how great the pressure on schools, hospitals and housing becomes, or how much wages in our poorest communities are pushed down' (BBC News, 2016). Prominent pro-Leave campaigner, then Foreign Secretary and future Prime Minister, Boris Johnson, said that exiting the European Union was the only means to curb mass immigration (BBC News, 2016).

It is no coincidence that, after the decision to leave the European Union was announced, a spate of xenophobic attacks and incidents swept the UK (Komaromi & Singh, 2016). As well as targeting White Europeans, a sharp increase in racist hate crime was levelled towards long-standing former Commonwealth citizens (Virdee & McGeever, 2018). It became clear that some British people felt that the vote to leave the EU permitted them to act out racist views and beliefs: 'The EU referendum result has perhaps emboldened racists by leading them to believe that the majority agree with their views on immigration and legitimising such public expressions of hatred' (*The Guardian*, 2016).

Benson and Lewis (2019) undertook a study to understand what Brexit means to British people of colour living in 8 of the 27 EU countries and found that the Brexit referendum had brought racism and xenophobia to the surface in a manner that was sanctioned by the state.

'What has transpired in Britain since the Leave campaign won has only shown how easily the veneer of civility and conviviality can be peeled back to reveal the virulence of racism and xenophobia seething under the skin of British social life' (Khalili, 2017:253). The responses highlighted the 'longstanding exclusionary operations of Britishness, by which people of colour are denied the right to belong' in a Britain in which structural and systemic racism is embedded and where racial exclusion, discrimination, and racism are 'business as usual' (Benson & Lewis, 2019:2228).

It could be concluded from Benson and Lewis (2019) that there is an underlying narrative that Black people should only operate on the fringes and margins of society and should be grateful they are here; racism and discrimination should be accepted, and Black people should not complain because the UK is better than where they came from. In other words, we should be grateful – what's the problem?

The notion of belittling, othering and indifference towards Black populations was brought to the fore when the Windrush scandal first came to light in 2014, whereby it transpired that thousands of established Caribbean-born British residents were treated as illegal immigrants and denied the right to work, benefits or healthcare. Several Black residents were improperly apprehended or even deported from the UK.

Campaigners raised concerns with the Home Office but were met with denial (Webber & Edmond-Pettitt, 2018). It is argued that 'actions of the government in trying to deport Black Caribbean people whose citizenship was held in question due to governmental conspiracy or incompetency was but the sharp end of a continuum' of the racialisation of Black people through historic oppression (Reddie, 2020:81), suggesting the existence of a stealth approach to targeting Black populations that were viewed as dispensable and powerless. In April 2018, escalating protests over the Windrush scandal by anti-racist campaigners and victims forced the Conservative Home Secretary Amber Rudd to resign.

The approach of racially profiling a seemingly easy target of random individual Black people and quietly removing them from the country in the dead of night spectacularly backfired (Reddie, 2020). The furore and sense of outrage of ordinary British people in the UK in response to the government's desire to deport established Caribbean immigrants galvanised the media and action groups in a positive way. Reddie asserts that the 'virulently racist treatment meted out to Black people of the Windrush Generation' is even more revolting because 'it exacerbates the already pernicious nature of being "othered" in a nation that often wants to exemplify homogeneity and sameness', causing Black people to 'remain at the bottom of the socio-economic ladder' (2020:81).

The response to this inequality was strengthened by universal condemnation in the face of blatant racially motivated immigration practices. Brexit and Windrush provide pertinent insights into the othering of Black and ethnically diverse people in the UK and the antecedents of treatment as it relates to integration and the construction of identity. This phenomenon further manifested in the Black Lives Matter movement and the COVID-19 pandemic which will be discussed in the next chapter.

Summary

We have explored the history of Black people in the UK and how critical race theory can help us understand how racism is woven into society and normalised. We've also taken a deeper look at immigration and integration. We learned that Black people were invited to the UK but then faced the harsh reality of life on the bottom rung of the ladder.

When I think of my maternal grandparents arriving in the UK for the first time and the harsh reception they received, it makes me shudder. There's no sugar-coating the racism and hostility and, as time goes on, the type of racism changes but it doesn't go away. It seems to mutate and form and reform, so we must remain ever-vigilant and stay one step ahead.

CHAPTER 2

UNVEILING THE UGLY TRUTH

Not everything that is faced can be changed,
but nothing can be changed until it is faced.

James Baldwin

Workplace Culture and Career Progression of Black Professionals

As discussed in the previous chapter, the use of the term BAME (Black Asian and minority ethnic) to describe non-White employees is common when describing Black and Asian employees in the UK workplace. However, grouping together ethnically diverse people can have the effect of masking the more severe racially discriminatory experiences of Black people.

To elucidate this point, despite Black Asian and racially diverse people constituting 18% of the UK population, there is a significant disparity in the representation of Black people in leadership roles as distinct from other ethnicities. According to Wyatt and Silvester (2015), only 1.5% of senior positions on boards in the UK are held by Black individuals, with little to no increase in the number of managers, directors and top-level officials since 2014. These figures remain similar in 2024, ten years later (Parker, 2024).

In the UK, 30% of the workforce is employed in the public sector, particularly in areas such as education and healthcare. This sector has the highest percentage of workers compared to other industries. Among these workers, 44% are Black, which is the highest representation of any ethnic group (Office for National Statistics, 2020).

Despite this, Black representation at senior levels has either remained stagnant or declined. This trend can be observed across many public sector institutions, indicating persistent slow progress.

The gap between the unemployment rate of Black workers and White workers is significant, with Black unemployed at a rate of 7.7% of all employees, compared to 3.3% of White workers in unemployment, more than twice the rate (House of Commons Library, 2024). In addition to the lower employment rate, despite having a number of professional qualifications, Black employees are not being promoted as frequently as White employees.

The Race at Work: Black Voices report (2020), compiled by Business in the Community, shows that White employees are more likely to work in all-White teams and that, despite Black employees having higher qualifications and valuing career progression, this does not translate into equal opportunities for promotion and advancement. These findings highlight persistent biases in employment policies and practices. Additionally, the report discovered that ethnically diverse employees rely more on recruitment agencies but have less faith in the fairness of their treatment, suggesting that recruitment agencies play a key role in perpetuating bias and discrimination in hiring practices.

Nepotism plays a role in these biased recruitment patterns also. Nepotism in recruitment refers to the practice of favouring relatives, friends or close associates when hiring or promoting individuals within an organisation, regardless of their qualifications or suitability for the role. This form of preferential treatment undermines merit-based hiring processes, potentially excluding more qualified or deserving candidates. Nepotism has created a culture of inequality and lower employee morale, and has eroded trust in leadership, as it often prioritises personal connections over skills, experience and competence.

Eight years ago, the Runnymede Trust (2017:6) reported on the challenges faced by ethnically diverse women in the labour market, who faced both sexism and racism. The report found that discrimination and bias exist at every stage of the recruitment process, from evaluating CVs and applications to the interview and after being hired. The report concluded that blind CVs are not effective, workplace equality policies are failing, and structural racism is present and expressed through personal prejudices in the workplace.

A year later, the Lammy report (2017) also found widespread disparities in the treatment of Black and ethnically diverse individuals in the criminal justice system and emphasised the importance of employment in promoting a law-abiding life and reforming offenders. These reports emphasise the ongoing inequality in British society. However, little progress has been made since then.

More than a third of the UK's top listed companies missed the Parker report's (2016) target of having at least one Black Asian and minority ethnic director by 2021 (Parker, 2020).

The data did improve by 2022, however, with 96 of the 100 FTSE companies meeting the target. This data remained the same in 2024 (Parker Review, 2024). The representation in FTSE 250 organisations was lacking, with 69% having no ethnically diverse directors (Parker, 2020; Kinder, 2020). FTSE 250 companies currently have 13.5% ethnically diverse board members (Parker Review, 2024).

Despite this progress, as highlighted in the first section, only 1% of FTSE 100 directors are Black, and in the FTSE 250 less than 2% of director roles are held by Black employees (Parker Review, 2024). It is important to understand these workplace racial diversity patterns across the UK, as they reflect societal norms.

These findings and countless studies demonstrate that discrimination is a pervasive problem in the UK labour market (West, 2025). The culture that enables these practices is ever present in many organisations. Yet, it can be difficult to raise concerns due to the practices and behaviour in UK organisations. In the UK, many British people refrain from showing emotion; this is known as the 'stiff upper lip' culture and refers to a stoic attitude of emotional restraint and resilience in the face of adversity. This cultural trait developed during the Victorian era and reached its peak in the first half of the twentieth century.

It is characterised by maintaining composure, suppressing emotional displays and facing challenges with quiet determination. It was reinforced through literature, public schools and wartime experiences, becoming a symbol of the British character. In recent decades, this cultural norm has begun to soften, with more open emotional expression becoming increasingly accepted in British society. However, the stiff upper lip culture still bubbles below the surface, dictating what behaviour is acceptable and unacceptable. This may offer a partial clue as to why it is so difficult for employees to raise concerns and achieve successful non-career-ending outcomes.

The Ethnicity Pay Gap

The issue of pay disparity between ethnically diverse and White staff in the UK has been a major topic of debate in the field of organisational discrimination. This led to the creation of the ethnicity pay gap measurement (McGregor-Smith, 2017). The Trades Union Congress (TUC) reported that ethnically diverse employees were facing a growing pay gap compared to White employees (Eddo-Lodge, 2018).

Despite being a government-commissioned report, the recommendation made by the McGregor-Smith (2017) review to publish ethnicity pay gaps was still under consideration by the government three years later (Byrne et al., 2020), seven years after its production, and to date has still not been enacted. Whilst the current Labour government has outlined proposals to introduce new legislation, which is discussed later, the continued existence of the ethnicity pay gap highlights the ongoing issues of discrimination and unequal treatment of Black and ethnically diverse employees in the workplace.

Research by the Trades Union Congress in 2018 suggested at the time that there was a 23% gap in hourly pay between Black and White workers. Black people with A-levels were paid 14% less on average than White workers with equivalent qualifications, while public sector workers in London faced a deficit of 37.5%. Recent data shows that people in the UK from the Black 'other' ethnic group had the lowest average earnings one year after graduating, earning £19,400, followed by Black Caribbean people who earned £19,800 (Ethnicity Facts and Figures, 2023).

The potential gain for the UK economy referred to in the introduction of £24 billion annually accounts for 1.3% of GDP (McGregor-Smith, 2017). Imagine that – the UK economy could grow by 1.3%, and all we have to do is not be racist! Nonetheless, studies reveal that emphasising the economic benefits of addressing discrimination through the business case approach has been insufficient to bring about change and this results in calls for a new method.

According to the McGregor-Smith review, which analysed the challenges faced by Black and ethnically diverse individuals in the UK workplace, discrimination and prejudice were present throughout their entire careers and even prior to them. The review noted that this issue was prevalent in areas like networking, recruitment and the workplace itself (Race in the Workplace, 2017:3). However, the McGregor-Smith review one year on (Business in the Community, 2018) showed that little progress had been made in regard to the proposed solutions in the 2017 review.

These findings indicate a systemic issue in tackling workplace discrimination and highlight the need for greater transparency in career progression opportunities and a stronger emphasis on equity and inclusion policies that are implemented effectively. The lack of access to information and role models for ethnically diverse employees can lead to limited advancement and perpetuates a cycle of underrepresentation at senior levels within the workplace.

The wealth of qualitative and quantitative data further supports the need for increased action to address the disparities and bridge the gap in opportunities between Black and White British workers.

The ethnicity pay gap in London is 22.5%, but for Black employees the pay gap is over 33% (Greater London Authority, 2024). Despite an emphasis on equality and diversity and organisational compliance with equality legislation, huge inequalities and disparities pervade the labour market in terms of salaries, recruitment and promotions (Parks-Yancy, 2006; Avery, 2011; Ossenkop et al., 2015; Bhopal, 2018).

Tackling racial discrimination requires government intervention through legislation and cultural change; however, measures taken to date have proved to be inadequate (ACAS, 2006; CIPD, 2017). Moreover, these measures have been found to 'ignore the power imbalance between individual employees and employers' (Seifert & Wang, 2018:2). Ethnically diverse employees believe that discrimination stagnates their career progression (CIPD, 2017) and McGregor-Smith's (2017) solution of increasing representation has been criticised for being outdated (Seifert & Wang, 2018).

A study by Wang and Seifert (2020) found that the lack of representation and pay disparities faced by ethnically diverse employees in the UK workplace are due to systemic discrimination and racism. They found that Black staff have a lower perception of fair pay and equal treatment in the workplace compared to their White colleagues. This highlights the need for effective measures to be taken by both the government and organisations to address these disparities.

The Equality Act (2010) has faced criticism for not keeping pace with modern forms of racism, including microaggressions and structural racism (Heath & DiStasio, 2019; Miller, 2020a).

Although the Equality Act (2010) makes discrimination illegal based on race or ethnicity, it has not ensured better outcomes. The lack of monitoring systems by the government to examine compliance with the race equality duty by educational institutions has also been criticised (Miller, 2020a).

There is a need for the Equality Act (2010) to be updated to effectively address racial discrimination in the workplace (Miller, 2020a) and it is argued that this should apply across all sectors. Whilst the Labour government have introduced the draft Equality (Race and Disability) Bill (discussed later), it is yet to be seen whether the changes will go far enough.

Identity and Racism

It can be argued that race plays a significant role in British society, leading to discrimination, racism, injustice and stereotyping that persist and influence societal structures. Sociologists acknowledge the impact of racial logics and frames of reference, recognising the way they are utilised in daily interactions. For Black individuals, the colour of their skin is often the first identifier, putting race at the forefront of daily experiences.

The construction of Blackness in society is rooted in racism and prejudice, with Black people being viewed as symbols of powerlessness and poverty. This global issue of hatred for darker-skinned people is perpetuated by the association of whiteness with power and money, while poverty is seen as blackening. This has led to the historic subjugation and othering of Black people, which continues to this day in the form of suppression in the workplace. The satisfaction derived from knowing that there is always a group of people worse off, originating from the antecedents of White supremacy, only reinforces this tendency.

Anti-Black racism is a unique form of racism faced by Black individuals. Eddo-Lodge (2018) sheds light on the racial disparity between different ethnic groups and how Black individuals face more severe discrimination at various stages of their lives. This includes being excluded in schools, facing a degree attainment gap, having lower chances of being admitted to prestigious Russell Group universities, facing discrimination in the graduate workforce, being over-policed, receiving harsher sentences, and being overrepresented in mental health diagnosis and detention.

To categorise all Black and ethnically diverse people as one unified group is to overlook the intense discrimination faced by Black people and fails to acknowledge the multiple and targeted forms of discrimination they experience.

Anti-Black racism is a persistent issue that is rooted in the historical context of slavery, colonialism and White supremacy. The manifestation of anti-Black racism can be seen in the racial disparities experienced by Black people in various aspects of their lives.

According to Ross (2020), anti-Blackness is described as a theoretical framework that highlights society's failure to acknowledge Black people's humanity, and instead displays disdain, disregard and disgust towards them. This disdain is evident in the UK through the lack of concern for Black people's specific struggles and mistreatment, as well as the inadequate updating of equality laws to address the numerous forms of racial discrimination.

The failure to acknowledge the specific experience of Black people and the failure to update equality legislation to adequately address racial discrimination has contributed to the disregard for the humanity of Black people. Black men are still viewed as the ultimate "other".

Busey and Coleman-King (2020) argue that anti-Black systemic racism is a global issue originating from worldwide White supremacy, and that the solidarity among Black citizens across nations is frequently not discussed in educational settings (Busey & Coleman-King, 2020). This lack of discussion leads to fear of Black people joining together to combat oppression, and society's resistance to altering its distorted and racist structures.

It is argued that anti-Black racism needs to be framed in systemic terms and the impact of British identity commitments on institutional, social and personal racism must be recognised. The British identity is believed to be an anti-Black institution, whereas it should be a central component of efforts to eliminate it.

The concept of British identity as an anti-Black institution (Beckles-Raymond, 2020) is crucial to understanding what it means to be British. It has been noted that right-wing politicians use fears and stereotypes about Blackness during significant events, such as elections or referendums, to tap into the underlying racism in society.

Jaspal et al.'s study (2020) of British national identity and life satisfaction in ethnically diverse people found that 'ethnic minority' groups in the UK should not be considered as a homogeneous group and promoting their wellbeing should acknowledge their differences.

The study also found that racial discrimination negatively affects the formation of a British national identity and limits life satisfaction, whereas promoting a civic British national identity that includes ethnic diversity leads to a greater sense of identity. In other words, Black and ethnically diverse people want to feel part of the fabric of British society rather than being mistreated because of the colour of their skin.

Marginalised groups have long been made to feel inferior by racism and its consequences, which have been defined by those in power over them. These definitions have their roots in European science, where people were first categorised based on skin colour, leading to a long history of poor treatment for ethnically diverse people.

To resist this fate, Black and ethnically diverse groups have tried to reject the inferior worth assigned to them by racial concepts. In his book *Black Skin, White Masks*, Frantz Fanon (1967) claimed that the colour of his skin trapped him in a situation not of his own making. This is still the case today, nearly 60 years later.

In response, Black people have sought to resist the negative connotations of race, through movements like Black power or consciousness. These movements aimed to challenge the notion of White dominance and suppression of the Black race. There is a complicated relationship between feeling proud of Black identity and the historical association of Blackness with oppression. The idea that White people must always be at the centre is a significant issue that hinders the creation of a level playing field where all are equal and there is no dominant group.

Racial Tensions

The murders of Breonna Taylor and George Floyd in the USA in 2020 sparked global protests in support of the Black Lives Matter (BLM) movement, drawing attention to the issue of racial discrimination and police brutality against African Americans. The UK was not immune to the issue of racism, as evidenced by the Brixton uprising, the Stephen Lawrence murder, the Grenfell Tower fire and the Windrush scandal.

The BLM protests in the UK in 2020 were seen as a culmination of years of systemic racism in areas such as workplace discrimination, police brutality, immigration policies and the unequal impact of the COVID-19 pandemic, leading to calls for change and greater awareness of the issues. The protests were one of the largest anti-racist movements since the slavery abolition movement, leading to corporate apologies and commitments for reparations for connections to colonialism and the slave trade.

Some of the notable examples include Lloyds of London (global insurance business) and Greene King (pub retailer and brewer) apologising for their role in the slave trade, Aviva (insurance business) apologising for its connection to the slave trade, Cass Business School (City St George's, University of London) changing its name to Bayes Business School to disassociate from Sir John Cass's links to slavery, the Bank of England apologising for the slavery involvement of previous governors and directors, and Oxford University finally recommending the removal of colonialist Cecil Rhodes' statue from Oriel College after sustained protests, but later backtracking and installing a plaque next to the statue instead.

The protests brought increased attention to the experiences of Black people in the UK and globally and led to corporate reflection and apology for connections to slavery and colonialism. As a result, Black employees started to share their experiences of racial discrimination in the workplace and began to highlight the gap between corporate diversity and inclusion policies and their actual experiences. This brought attention to the ongoing issue of racial discrimination in the workplace and the need for meaningful change and action.

The BLM movement was successful in raising awareness about racial inequality, police brutality and systemic racism, inspiring important conversations and driving change in various societies, including the UK. However, the changes prompted by the movement faced backlash in some communities, with the emergence of counter-slogans such as 'White Lives Matter' (WLM) and far-right groups opposing its message. Critics argue that BLM's focus on racial inequality is divisive and undermines social cohesion. Misinformation and distortion of BLM's message led to confusion and misunderstanding, with some people perceiving BLM as advocating for the superiority of one race over another, rather than promoting racial equality and justice.

The opposition to BLM, particularly through groups promoting WLM and far-right ideologies, has caused harm in various ways. These groups and movements contributed to increased racial tensions and sometimes led to incidents of violence and unrest. Protests and counter-protests occasionally turned violent, as witnessed in the far-right rally in London in June 2020. This rally, ostensibly organised to protect historical monuments targeted by some BLM protesters, resulted in violent clashes with police and counter-protesters, highlighting the potential for violence when the backlash against BLM is left unchecked.

Black people are often called upon to comment on issues related to racism and are then criticised for being overly sensitive, ungrateful, easily offended or not understanding satire. Examples of this approach can be seen with public figures such as Meghan Markle and Stormzy. Meanwhile, the former Home Secretary, Priti Patel, labelled the Black Lives Matter protests as 'dreadful' and disagreed with 'taking the knee'[2] (Parveen, 2021).

[2] 'Taking the knee' is a symbolic gesture against racism on the football pitch.

Despite these challenges, the Black Lives Matter movement remains committed to its mission of dismantling systemic racism, advocating for racial justice and fostering a more just and equal society. It is essential for individuals and communities to continue supporting and amplifying the voices of Black people and to challenge the harmful narratives perpetuated by racist groups.

The COVID-19 Pandemic

If climbing the rough side of the mountain was not arduous enough, the COVID-19 pandemic also had a disproportionate impact on Black employees in the UK. According to the Office for National Statistics, Black people were more likely to work in industries such as healthcare, hospitality and retail, all of which were hit hardest by the pandemic. They were also more likely to work in roles that were deemed essential but offered less protection from the virus, such as public transportation and environmental services. Therefore, the COVID-19 pandemic was experienced more acutely by the Black population in the UK.

There were high death rates among Black and South Asian communities (Haynes, 2020). A report by Public Health England (2020) found that ethnically diverse communities were at a higher risk of dying from COVID-19, with the risk highest for Black people. These disparities were further exacerbated by existing inequalities, such as poor housing and overcrowding, lack of access to adequate healthcare, high levels of poverty, and a dependence on public transport. The disproportionate impact of the pandemic on ethnically diverse communities in the UK highlights the need for greater action to address systemic inequalities and to ensure that everyone has equal access to health and social care.

The Runnymede report of 2020 also confirmed that Black and ethnically diverse individuals were disproportionately affected by severe illness and death caused by COVID-19. This was due to a combination of factors, such as their occupation of key worker positions, and lack of access to proper protective equipment in the workplace.

It is important to note the factors that led to Black people taking up essential roles. Firstly, historically, Black communities have faced systemic barriers to higher education, wealth accumulation, and entry into certain professional fields due to discrimination and segregation. After slavery, Black people were often relegated to labour-intensive or service-oriented roles.

This pattern, though evolving, has had lasting implications. Secondly, there are economic considerations such as job accessibility (essential roles in healthcare and transportation often require certification or training rather than advanced degrees, making them more accessible to individuals with limited access to higher education) and also job stability as these roles tend to offer relatively stable employment and benefits, which are attractive in communities where economic disparities may limit access to generational wealth or entrepreneurial opportunities.

Further, the veer towards essential roles also stems from cultural values and community impact, in that commitment to service sits well with Black communities' desire to contribute to the wellbeing of others, particularly through healthcare and public service roles.

The relationship between socio-economic indicators, such as income, social class, occupation and educational attainment, and poor health outcomes among ethnically diverse populations were amplified during the pandemic. For example, Black people have a household income that is 37% lower than the national average. To address these inequalities, employers need to be held accountable for their harmful employment practices in relation to Black people which result in lower wages.

Black people are often underrepresented in secure, well-paying jobs, and instead are overrepresented in front-line roles, which placed them at a higher risk of contracting and dying from COVID-19. These inequalities were literally having a deadly impact on Black communities. The COVID-19 pandemic heavily affected the shut-down sectors, with a significant number of Black employees being impacted.

According to the House of Commons (2020), 11.5% of Black and ethnically diverse workers and 12% of all workers are employed in these sectors, with ethnically diverse employees making up 28% of the vulnerable jobs in the transport sector and 16% of the vulnerable jobs in the accommodation and food service sector.

The financial impact of the pandemic has also been felt more by ethnically diverse people, as shown by a Business Management Group (BMG) poll commissioned by the *Independent* (2020), where 46% of Black and ethnically diverse people's household income decreased due to the virus, against a 28% decrease for White households. Black and ethnically diverse respondents also had a higher job loss rate of 15%, compared to 8% of White British households. This financial impact is likely to have long-lasting effects on the Black community and could further deepen the existing discrimination, health inequality and economic disparity.

Recent UK Events

Recent events in the UK have illuminated racial divisions and how they manifest in society. In December 2020, a 15-year-old Black schoolgirl, known as Child Q, was subjected to a strip search by Metropolitan Police officers at her school in Hackney, East London. Child Q was wrongly suspected of possessing cannabis by school staff. She was removed from an exam and taken to the school's medical room. Two female police officers conducted a strip search, with no appropriate adult present. The girl was menstruating and forced to remove her sanitary towel. No drugs were found during the search. The incident sparked widespread outrage and investigations into police practices.

A safeguarding review found the search was unjustified and racism was 'likely' a factor. The incident led to calls for a review of police strip search powers. It highlighted issues of 'adultification bias' affecting Black children. The case prompted investigations into strip searches of children across England and Wales. The Child Q case brought attention to the disproportionate impact of police practices on Black children and the need for significant reforms in how law enforcement interacts with minors in school settings (*Independent*, 2023). Although two of the three police officers involved were dismissed, this action occurred five years after the incident, and alarmingly, the misconduct panel concluded that ethnicity was not a factor". As the mother of two beautiful Black female children, I was absolutely appalled to learn of this case and felt it was a stark reminder of the second-class treatment meted out to Black children in the UK, who are often not treated as children. Along with the blatant racism, the disregard for human rights was palpable.

This shocking example is not the only issue Black children have to contend with. Black children in the UK face significant barriers that impact their educational and future career prospects. Further research highlights systemic racism and teachers' low expectations as major contributors to the academic underachievement of Black Caribbean children (Demie & McLean, 2017; Okuwa, as cited in Black Equity Organisation, 2024). These systemic barriers, combined with institutional racism, result in a lack of diversity and representation in educational settings, exacerbating the issue (Wallace & Joseph-Salisbury, 2022; Black Equity Organisation, 2024). Black students are disproportionately excluded from schools, leading to poor educational attainment and increased vulnerability to negative outcomes (Institute for Public Policy Research & The Difference, 2024). Furthermore, the absence of diverse role models and inadequate career guidance hinder Black children's ability to envision and pursue various career paths (Institute of Education, 2024).

These systemic barriers profoundly affect the educational trajectory of Black children, leading to a complex array of disadvantages. By the time they enter the workforce, many will have already navigated significant obstacles. Unfortunately, this cycle of discrimination often persists in the professional sphere, where the exhaustion and frustration can be overwhelming. The relentless continuation of these challenges underscores the urgent need for systemic change.

The Euro 2020 final (held in 2021 due to COVID-19 delays) between England and Italy was marred by a wave of racist abuse directed at England players Marcus Rashford,

Jadon Sancho and Bukayo Saka after they missed penalties in the shootout loss. Over 600 reports of racist comments were received by the UK Football Policing Unit (UKFPU) and Twitter removed more than 1,900 racist, abusive tweets in the wake of the final. Most tweets originated from UK accounts (BBC News, 2021).

The incident highlighted ongoing issues of racism in football and online spaces and the abuse extended beyond players, with reports of racist abuse directed at schoolchildren linked to the match. The incident brought renewed attention to the persistent problem of racial abuse in football and the need for coordinated efforts from authorities, social media companies, and society to combat this issue (*Independent*, 2023). The treatment of these Black players was another indication of the racism lurking in British society, which bubbles to the surface at times, but is always there.

The Commission on Race and Ethnic Disparities, whose findings were published in a report in March 2021 under the then Conservative government, was chaired by Dr Tony Sewell. Dr Sewell is a Black educational consultant and former teacher who has worked in education reform and addressing disparities in academic achievement among ethnically diverse groups.

The report, often referred to as the Sewell report, sparked significant debate and controversy for its conclusions, particularly its assertion that institutional racism was not a systemic issue in the UK. It emphasised socio-economic, cultural and familial factors as key drivers of disparities, which led to mixed reactions from various stakeholders and communities.

This positioning fuelled allegations that the government was using Dr Sewell's racial identity to reinforce its narrative, which many activists, scholars and community leaders viewed as minimising the lived experiences of Black and ethnically diverse people. The report's framing and conclusions were widely criticised as an example of 'gaslighting' ethnically diverse communities, with opponents asserting that it denied the structural and systemic roots of racial inequalities in areas such as policing, education and employment.

The conclusions of the report were widely criticised by various groups, including being condemned by UN Human Rights advocates who surfaced the intention to normalise White supremacy and further listed 20 stakeholders who dissociated themselves from its conclusions.

The report's findings were also challenged by Members of Parliament, trade unions, and equality campaigners who argued that the report downplayed structural racism (Guardian, 2021), ignored the lived experiences of Black and ethnically diverse people, and failed to address the root causes of discrimination and bias in career progression.

The lack of consequences for failing to act further exacerbates the problem, leaving employers with little incentive to make changes that would address biased practices, culture and policy. The report could be seen as continuing the pattern of racism denial in the UK (Royal College of General Practitioners, 2021) and is offensive to Black and ethnically diverse people facing daily discrimination. I was astounded at this report and, quite frankly, its conclusions are not only inept but are an egregious falsehood.

Following the murder of Sarah Everard by a serving Metropolitan Police officer, the Casey Review led by Baroness Louise Casey, published on 21 March 2023, provided a comprehensive and damning report on the Metropolitan Police Service (the Met) in London which exposed deep-rooted issues within

Britain's largest police force (Baroness Casey Review, 2023). The review concluded that the Met is institutionally racist, misogynist and homophobic (Police Foundation, 2023). It found widespread bullying, with a fifth of staff and officers with protected characteristics having experienced bullying (*Independent*, 2023).

The cultural issues highlighted a rife 'boys' club' culture where discrimination was tolerated and 'baked into the system' (Casey Review: One Year On, 2024); a culture of silence and complicity with personal incentives to keep quiet about misconduct was also emphasised. In addition, one in ten female officers reported being sexually harassed or assaulted by colleagues, misconduct cases were shown to take a long time to be resolved, and there were racial disparities in the misconduct system, with Black officers dealt with more harshly than White officers.

The review made 16 recommendations for significant changes and reform. Whilst the new Met leadership, including Commissioner Sir Mark Rowley, accepted the findings and acknowledged the need for radical reform, one year after the review's publication concerns remain about the pace and extent of change within the Met, with issues experienced by staff from ethnic backgrounds persisting (Desai, 2024). Is it any wonder that there is mistrust in the police on the part of the Black community, with the failure to change culture being such a topical issue?

In 2020, 21-year-old trainee firefighter Jaden Francois-Esprit tragically took his own life, raising serious concerns about racism and discrimination within the London Fire Brigade. His family alleged that he faced bullying and a hostile work environment at Wembley Fire Station due to his race, contributing to his mental health struggles. An independent investigation commissioned by the LFB found insufficient evidence of direct discrimination but acknowledged organisational failings in supporting Jaden. His death prompted broader scrutiny of the LFB's culture, culminating in a 2022 independent review led by Nazir Afzal, which declared the brigade 'institutionally misogynist and racist', citing widespread bullying and discrimination. It is both worrying and disappointing that cases like these are still happening and that cultures are not changing fast enough to ensure it does not happen again.

In amongst these controversies, the 'cost-of-living crisis' entered the UK vernacular in late 2021 and refers to the fall in disposable income for households due to the rapid rise in food and energy costs combined with high inflation and rising interest rates (Institute for Government, 2023). In a nutshell, wages have not kept up with inflation. As Black people are overrepresented amongst the lowest-income groups, they faced greater risk of redundancies during the crisis, with many worried about losing their job due to rising costs (Runnymede, 2022).

According to a Runnymede report (2022), the cost-of-living crisis had a disproportionate and severe impact on Black people who are 2.5 times more likely to be in relative poverty than their White counterparts. The cost-of-living crisis intensified prevailing racial inequalities, with people of African and Caribbean descent facing more severe financial difficulty, declining health outcomes and amplified discrimination (Runnymede, 2022). This has contributed to a growing economic gap of Black people in the UK (University of Leeds, 2022).

A study by Drydakis (2024) found Black people experienced a 4.45% decrease in general health and a 5.62% decrease in mental health during the crisis. Starkly, cases of discrimination were related to a 26.4% decline in general health and a 27.1% decline in mental health. Disturbingly, the study found that discrimination towards Black people increased by 3.75% during the 2022/23 cost-of-living crisis, with rising inflation being associated with a 2.9% increase in discrimination towards Black people. This represents a double bind of cost-of-living pressures and discrimination – a negative mix at an already difficult time.

With these issues festering, sadly, a mass stabbing occurred in Southport in Merseyside, a seaside town in Northwest England on 29 July 2024. Three White children were killed. After this incident, false claims circulated online by far-right groups that the perpetrator of the attack was a Muslim asylum seeker. In addition, there was growing Islamophobic, racist and anti-immigrant sentiments being expressed online and in far-right rhetoric.

As a result, from 30 July to 5 August 2024, far-right, anti-immigration protests and riots occurred in England and Northern Ireland. The unprecedented violent rampage included racist attacks, arson and looting. The newly elected Labour government took action to utilise policing and legal powers to arrest and charge the perpetrators (*Observer*, 2024).

The anarchy spread far and wide, and people from Black and ethnically diverse backgrounds feared for their safety. Videos emerged of far-right mobs blockading roads in Middlesbrough and only allowing White drivers through (*Mirror*, 2024). I remember contemplating whether it would be safe to visit the gym in the evening, as there were reports of far-right protesters expected in Northwest London. During this time, organisations were thinking about the best way to keep employees safe.

In my organisation, we held a listening session for employees and offered support. It was a tense and unsettling experience, a further reminder that racism looms large and rears its head when the opportunity arises. It was also a reminder that there is a different experience for those who are visibly different and can be more easily targeted by racist attacks.

An independent report on the Inclusion at Work Panel's recommendations for improving diversity and inclusion (D&I) practice in the workplace was published in 2024, under the Sunak Conservative government. The panel was chaired by Pamela Dow and recommended a framework for embedding evidence-informed D&I practice utilising three criteria: 1) gathering evidence systematically and comprehensively; 2) putting evidence into practice; and 3) reviewing interventions and processes regularly.

The report outlined three conditions for success: board- and CEO-level direction and leadership, awareness and mitigation of unintended consequences, and applying equality law correctly.

However, subsequently, the incoming Labour government set out the draft Equality (Race and Disability) Bill in the King's Speech (2024) which commits to introducing ethnicity pay gap reporting for large employers and gives Black and ethnically diverse employees the same protections as women now receive. The new law would treat equal pay claims based on ethnicity and disability on a par with existing protections for women. The proposed Act includes provisions against 'dual discrimination', allowing individuals facing prejudice due to a combination of protected characteristics to file a single discrimination claim. For example, a Black woman could bring a claim based on both race and sex discrimination.

Further, the Employment Rights Bill introduces an obligation on employers not to permit harassment of their employees by third parties and to specify reasonable prevention steps (Government Assets Publishing Service, 2024). These steps are welcome, but the detail will need to be examined further as progress is made towards legislation. In my view, equality legislation needs to go further. I will share more about this in the final chapter.

Kemi Badenoch, a Black woman, was elected leader of the decimated Conservative Party in 2024. However, Badenoch's views on race made her appointment controversial for many progressive people and organisations. Badenoch strongly opposes critical race theory and its implementation in British institutions and believes that Britain is 'one of the best countries in the world in which to be black' (*The Spectator*, 2020).

Not surprisingly, Badenoch supports the discredited Commission on Race and Ethnic Disparities report (2021) that found no evidence of institutional racism and engages in racism denial by ignoring the lived experiences and structural and racial inequalities faced by Black people in the UK (The Conversation, 2024). Badenoch's views on race are worrying, to say the least, and are at odds with the findings in my research which highlight that the lived experience of Black employees is framed by Whiteness, racism and biased workplace cultures.

It would be remiss not to talk about the influence the media has on racism. The UK media contributes to racism by perpetuating stereotypes and framing narratives that disproportionately criminalise ethnically diverse communities. Sensationalist reporting often amplifies negative stereotypes, particularly against Black and Asian communities, harnessing biases that shape public perceptions and policy attitudes.

Headlines and coverage frequently emphasise race in ways that reinforce 'us versus them' divisions, while neglecting systemic issues such as inequality or institutional racism. Additionally, the lack of diversity in media organisations results in limited perspectives and reinforces a dominant narrative centred on White experiences. This combination perpetuates structural racism by normalising discriminatory attitudes and marginalising the voices and experiences of ethnically diverse communities.

In addition, documentaries by public service broadcasters often limit Black experiences to topics of race, racism, crime and music (Oteka, 2022 and BCU, 2022). Further, Oteka (2022) found that 78% of respondents thought the media's portrayal of ethnically diverse people promoted racism. Media portrayals can affect how non-Black audiences engage with Black people and even how Black people see themselves. This trend extends to entertainment media, where a lack of diversity in awards nominations has sparked campaigns like #OscarsSoWhite (Action for Children, 2024).

Less than a quarter of Black 4- to 18-year-olds in the UK believed they saw children that looked like them on television, resulting in young people turning towards social media (Action for Children, 2024).

This is a persistent issue, and Black characters are often subject to tokenism and negative portrayals; historically, racist caricatures and blackface were common in British entertainment, with some shows only recently removing such content. A 2023 report by the Black British Voices Project confirmed that systemic racism remains an obstacle in every sector studied.

Key points from the report found that 41% of survey respondents identify racism as the biggest barrier to young Black people's educational attainment; 95% believe that the national curriculum neglects Black lives and experiences; fewer than 2% believe educational institutions take racism seriously; 98% feel they have to compromise on who they are in their workplace; 90% of young Black people expect to experience racial prejudice as adults; 87% of Black Britons distrust the criminal justice system; and 90% object to anti-Black stereotyping on TV.

This situation is exacerbated by underrepresentation in media roles. The number of Black journalists in British newsrooms is significantly low, with only 15% of top editors in major UK news outlets being from non-White backgrounds (Reuters, 2021). Consequently, Black journalists often feel 'alone and unsupported' in newsrooms, with their ideas frequently rejected (Al-Kaisy, 2022).

Coverage of events like Black Lives Matter demonstrations and the treatment of Meghan Markle have raised questions about ongoing racism in UK media. Further, colourism remains an issue, with lighter-skinned Black individuals often favoured in media representations (Action for Children, 2024). Close to 70% of stories about Black young men and boys relate to crime, a higher figure than for young men and boys generally. Violent crime, murders, and gun and knife crime account for most crime coverage featuring Black young men and boys, often with little context or explanation (Oteka, 2022).

The limited range of positive roles and stories, coupled with persistent negative stereotyping, continues to be a significant issue that affects both public perception and the Black community's self-image. The public perception feeds into the problematic way Black people are treated at work. These findings collectively highlight the ongoing challenges in achieving fair and diverse representation of Black people in UK media.

The Sainsbury's Christmas advert in 2020 featuring a Black family sparked a significant backlash, highlighting ongoing racism in the UK. While the advert celebrated family togetherness and tradition, it faced a wave of racist comments online, with some viewers claiming the campaign did not represent them or accusing the supermarket chain of pandering to diversity (*Guardian*, 2020).

Sainsbury's stood by the advert, emphasising their commitment to inclusivity and celebrating the diversity of their customers and the UK population. The backlash underscored the discomfort some hold over authentic representation of Black families in mainstream media and sparked wider discussions about systemic racism, the role of brands in promoting inclusivity, and the need to challenge such prejudices. This impacts on treatment in the workplace.

Racial stereotypes in the media filter into the workplace and create stigmatisation of Black people. This can show up in beliefs that Black people are aggressive, that hair touching is OK, that racial banter/jokes should be tolerated, in addition to the plethora of negative lived experiences that will be covered in this book.

Between the politics, far-right hostility, policing issues, inadequate legislation, racism, economic and health disparities and negative media portrayal experienced by people of colour in the UK, there is much that needs to be done to tackle racial injustice.

Across the pond, the re-election of President Trump, along with the installation of his unelected 'advisor' Elon Musk, represents a challenging time. President Trump has declared a war on Diversity, Equity and Inclusion, which has led to a number of Federal US employees losing their jobs and several large corporations abandoning their Diversity, Equity and Inclusion programmes. The fact that two powerful White men have announced that organisations should not aim to be equitable and fair is a great example of what is meant by White privilege. Their actions explain it better than I could hope to articulate in this book. But unfortunately, as we know, when the US sneezes, we in the UK catch a cold ...

Summary

I have explored how racism manifests in workplace culture, lower pay, major events and everyday situations. Bias and discrimination seem to be baked into British society like a perfectly cooked racism cake. A sprinkling of ingredients that are not fit for human consumption, and yet, people of colour must eat a slice of this racism cake every day.

However, we do not wish to have our cake and eat it too, we merely wish for a slice of normal (racism-free) cake – I prefer carrot cake or rainbow cake myself. Perhaps, one day, progressing careers will feel like a piece of cake for all Black people.

So how do these racial flashpoints and societal issues find their way into the workplace? The next chapter explores the Black employee experience.

CHAPTER 3

THE DAILY HUSTLE – THE BLACK EMPLOYEES' WORKPLACE EXPERIENCE

We must accept finite disappointment, but we must never lose infinite hope.

Martin Luther King, Jr

Introduction

I felt it was important that the career journeys of Black people were captured. These are real people and what happens at work has a profound impact on our whole lives. As referred to in the introduction, my doctoral research utilised constructivist grounded theory as an effective method to capture experiences within the research. Employment issues have affected me in the same way as other Black people and this was an important factor, as it meant that lived experiences of career progression could be shared to create deep understanding and interpretation between me as the doctoral researcher and those who took part in the research.

Constructivist grounded theory was a useful tool in the effective development of theory, as it meant concepts and ideas could be tested. Finally, constructivist grounded theory allowed for the co-construction approach which enabled participants to articulate their views and solutions to career progression barriers.

This section explores the lived experiences of organisational culture through the lens of race, and career progression. It provides a comprehensive and nuanced understanding of the experiences of Black professionals in the UK workplace, highlighting the importance of addressing systemic barriers to career progression to create a more equitable and just workplace.

Through the accounts of the interviewees in the research conducted, you will gain insight into the daily realities of discrimination, microaggressions and other challenges that Black professionals face in the workplace.

In addition to sharing the participants' experiences, I share my perspectives and positions both as the doctoral researcher and author. To establish what is really happening inside organisations, the next section details the conversations I held with Black people about their career experiences.

Impact of Ethnicity on Career Progression

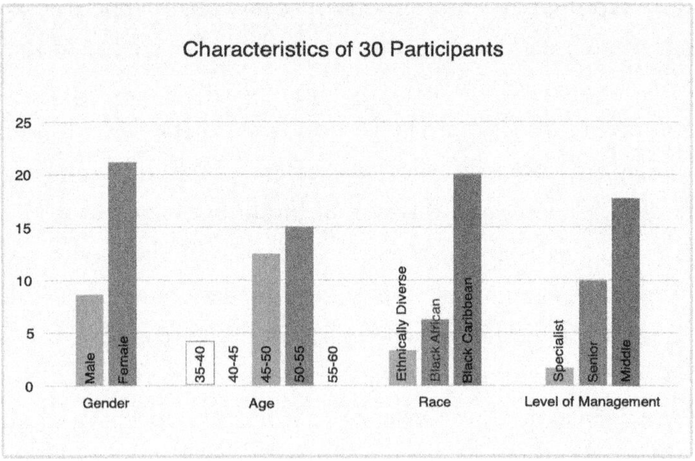

I carried out in-depth interviews with 30 Black professionals (Moncrieffe, 2021); the participants' characteristics are found in the appendix and depicted in the bar chart on page 68. The results of the interviews were staggering. Of these participants, 83% felt that their ethnicity had held them back in their careers, and 80% thought they had not achieved their full potential.

Collectively, they concurred on feeling stuck, facing a glass ceiling, and being held back for no reason other than the colour of their skin. They spoke about zigzag careers, having to leave organisations due to structural racism, and frequently moving from job to job. Many of the respondents had first degrees, Master's degrees and PhDs, and in some cases, had careers spanning several decades. I have used pseudonyms to anonymise the interviewees' identities.

I spoke to 'Mary' who is a mid-level manager in local government. Mary summed up much of what I heard from the group at large:

> *I think a lot of times when you are – looking at developing within an organisation; sometimes you feel you're held back because you don't know whether your senior leaders believe in you or not, and that can be quite disabling, and I've seen other groups of staff with different characteristics to mine who have been a bit more confident and brave to take those risks and have those conversations earlier on, whereas I didn't know that I could necessarily do that and I think I've tried to do that through proving my worth… I've seen other people get promoted over me, and I've felt a little bit put out where perhaps they've not had the same background that I've had.*

These situations are so dispiriting and draining. Black professionals also shared with me the obstacles they faced, such as not being given credit for their work, not being promoted for years, and their qualifications not being valued. Some felt that their careers suffered due to their ethnicity and background, including the way they spoke, their appearance and lack of social acceptance in workplace cultures built on the foundations of pubs and wine bars. They told me about the lack of leadership, sponsorship, allyship, advocacy and positive Black role models that made it even more challenging for them to progress in their careers. The multitude of hurdles faced can sometimes seem overwhelming and a heavy burden to carry above and beyond the actual day job that needs to be carried out to a high standard.

One male participant, 'Femi', worked at executive level in higher education and illustrated that progressing his career had come at huge personal sacrifice, including 60-hour weeks for several years. Femi described a lack of leadership and sponsorship and, most importantly, felt that there was a dearth of positive Black role models. Femi noted that he had 'no benchmark, nothing to really aspire to, nothing to really aim for' and felt that his career had stagnated but that at the same time he was working extremely hard, and noted:

> *and one thing my old boss once told me was if you want a job done, look for a busy man. So, the busier I was getting, the more was being piled on me. And I couldn't show any signs of wavering because then I think I would be falling into the stereotype of 'see, we knew they couldn't cope'.*

The absolute pressure felt here is palpable and speaks to the different level of performance expectations based on Black employees. Mary felt she was discriminated against not just by her ethnicity and gender but also by her class. She commented:

> *I feel like my career has been hindered by my class, by the way I speak and by the way I look. I do see myself to be successful, so it is not that I'm saying that that obviously has held me back. But I do believe that if I'd had the same leeway, the same opportunities as my counterparts, I'd probably be doing something even more advanced, even better.*

Reflecting on my own lived experience observations, White employees are given a chance to take on increasingly senior roles based on potential, whereas ethnically diverse employees are judged as a risk. Black professionals explained that this, at times, left them demoralised, with some describing applying for jobs up to 18 times unsuccessfully. Another professional observed that, in the NHS, ethnically diverse employees had to apply for senior roles ten times more before they were eventually successful.

The structural barriers applied different rules to ethnically diverse employees, creating higher and more challenging hurdles which made it difficult to progress in their careers. In essence, the interviewees faced a two-tier employee experience which was a direct result of their race. Sharma worked as an executive in a civil service quango; she had experienced a bumpy career of being held back and harassed by subordinates when she attained a senior management position in her previous role. Sharma noted:

> *Absolutely, one hundred million percent [it has taken me longer to achieve my career goals]. Everyone that went to Eton and Winchester – that is like the level below me or the same level as me – are in their early 30s, you know, they're like almost 20 years younger than me. And it was the same in the [broadcasting organisation]. It took me 8 years to get a management position and it took me 17 years to get to senior manager. That's not the case for other people.*

Think of the time wasted by taking so much longer to advance due to the colour of your skin; it's heartbreaking. The differences were stark when I compared their experiences to those of White employees. To achieve their career goals, they felt they had to be more qualified than their White peers to be in with a chance. Roland had worked in the NHS and was now an executive in the charity sector; he shared his observations on career progression:

> *I look at some of my White colleagues where we went to university together. I mean, one of them is working for Microsoft, another one is working for another big organisation, and when I look at them, I think to myself, surely by now, at this stage of my career, I should be somewhere much bigger. So, for me, that is probably something that's played on the back of my mind … when I look at my qualifications, these*

> *are just people with first degrees; I've got two Master's degrees. I've got coaching qualifications; I've got employment law qualifications, I've got ten years or more experience at board level, but these [White peers] are people with first [Bachelor] degrees, but they are flying the world.*

Roland was not bitter but was reflecting on missing out on the opportunity to fulfil his potential. The impact of watching those around you excel whilst racism is holding you back is excruciating.

Black professionals expressed a strong feeling that it would have been more difficult for them to achieve their current position if they had not studied. However, they felt that their White peers had become directors and chief executives in a short period of time, with fewer qualifications. Participants were thus articulating an unspoken rule that ethnically diverse employees had to be more qualified than their White peers just to get their foot in the door. In other words, a higher standard of educational attainment was being applied to global majority employees.

Black professionals reflected that they were subjected to different standards, whereby they were judged on the work they produced and past performance, whereas White colleagues were judged on their thoughts, comments and intellect. In other words, White employees were being judged on potential, whereas global majority employees were judged on prior experience. Femi felt that this unfair difference in the way ethnically diverse employees were assessed meant ethnically diverse employees did not have a clear career pathway, and he explained that:

> *I think for Black people, they have to formulate their own paths. Whereas everybody else follows a set path. You become a worker, you become a foreman, and you become a supervisor, you become a team manager, you become a Head of Service, you become a Director. That is a clear pathway for everybody else. I feel for Black people: we have to go in and out and around. And eventually, through years of experience, we end up in the positions we're in now. But that's just my experience … For me, there's been no clear, defined pathway to say right [redacted], if you gain these qualifications and you progress further, you work here for three years, you can become a Head of Service. From there, I can become a Group Director overseeing a number of services. Mine has been more out of chaos rather than design.*

The lack of support for career pathways was raised by Femi and is a critical issue. Black professionals described being stuck at the same level within organisations for many years with no prospect of promotion, or being demoted from their current roles. In my personal experience, I have witnessed new White line managers joining organisations and immediately demoting or dismissing Black employees in their team and replacing them with White employees. Black professionals resonated with these experiences and attributed these scenarios to White-dominated workplace cultures and widespread stereotyping and discrimination. Bunmi, a female senior professional in local government, felt she had had a difficult career, weaving in and out of different organisations due to racial discrimination and noted that, in terms of promotion, the person making the decision was:

> *more likely to choose people that are like themselves than, you know, anybody else. That would be the overriding overarching factor as opposed to just ability and capability ... I think we always have to work harder ... We always have to be smarter, wiser. We have to deliver more and better. Do I think it's the same? [career pathways]. Definitely not. No. And that's at any point in our careers. It's not just at any particular point, I think even at university it's the same. I think our career paths are always hard and long. And personally, for me, I know that my challenges are multiple-fold, not just to do with my ethnicity. And I accept that it's a choice I made. This is what I wanted to do, and I expected it. Not to the same extent it's presented itself. But I did expect it.*

The difficult and circuitous path for Black employees was a constant theme. This response evidenced that nepotism and the halo effect were a problem in organisational selection processes and beyond. In the context of racially biased recruitment, the halo effect can reinforce existing stereotypes and perpetuate systemic inequality. For instance, affinity bias may lead recruiters to favour candidates who share their own racial or cultural background, attributing positive qualities to these individuals while overlooking or undervaluing Black candidates. Black professionals expressed the view that success in job interviews increased if senior Black and ethnically diverse managers were represented on the recruitment selection panel and that, once in the role, they acquired powerful Black and ethnically diverse mentors and sponsors. The responses revealed unfair talent pipeline methods, which resulted in line managers providing

White colleagues with access to coveted assignments and projects to facilitate future promotions.

Black professionals surmised that White hiring managers colluded when roles became available at the exclusion of Black candidates. The Black professionals acknowledged that ethnically diverse employees were not regarded as top talent and were therefore expected to remain at lower levels. Participants observed ethnically diverse employees in low-grade roles receiving heavier workloads and being placed in geographical areas (for example, social workers) where there were more challenges.

These findings showed that Black people were being kept in a state of high stress, being required to constantly put in more effort whilst at the same time not being recognised for all the extra effort they were expending. The active collusion and unfair talent pipeline methods demonstrate that ethnically diverse employees are being deliberately blocked from career progression, which reinforces the critical race theory perspective of systemic racism woven into the fabric of institutions.

Interviewees described being overanalysed and receiving negative feedback from recruitment selection processes. They felt that constantly applying for promotions and being rejected was equivalent to trauma and believed that often Black and ethnically diverse candidates were only put forward to make up the numbers.

This is worrying, as it means their applications may be in vain and merely form part of a tick-box exercise. Where participants did successfully gain promotion up to board-level positions, this was typically due to having line managers or executive/board members who believed in them, rather than through formal talent and succession-planning mechanisms.

Participants expressed the view that some ethnically diverse employees had developed a complex in feeling that they were not valuable enough or not ready for promotion, due to the number of rejections they experienced. Participants felt that these lived experiences had been internalised for a long period of time and caused them to feel less confident in their abilities.

This resonated with my own experiences of career progression hurdles and the weariness felt. Marsha, a female executive working in the major building projects field, described the difficulty of being female in a male-dominated industry where she was clearly different from the hierarchy above her. Marsha gave an example from her previous role in the private sector where the clients only wanted to deal with White men. Marsha noted:

> *when I see my director, who is a White guy in his late 30s, I think my gosh if this is the director, all I need to do is become more confident when I speak because he doesn't know anything. So, I don't think I have reached the peak yet …*

Unfortunately, Marsha was describing an aspect of White privilege whereby average White people are able to excel but different standards are placed on Black employees. The Black professionals also spoke of a two-track system that deliberately shut Black employees out. They felt there was a mist-strewn path for Black employees compared to the clear way for White employees.

They also noted that racism in the workplace is often difficult to prove, and that ethnically diverse employees are not always believed when they describe what is occurring – particularly when these experiences involve micro-incivilities rather than the overt racism that was more commonly seen in the past. Lemar worked in the civil service and forged a successful career but felt it was difficult for Black professionals with integrity to succeed:

> *It is a fog and mist and hurdle-strewn path for Black staff compared to their White counterparts … the clear path that does exist, it exists for White people, it doesn't exist for Black people … for the Black person who is prepared to sell their mother, they can walk that path … But for most of us and certainly for those of us that are woke, including some White folks, we're not prepared to do that.*

Lemar was referring to the majority of decent Black people who have ethics and integrity, which means they would not trample over Black colleagues to climb the corporate ladder. Despite these challenges, some interviewees succeeded in gaining promotion, often due to the support of line managers or executive/board members who believed in them. But even then, the respondents noted that the problem with making comparisons is that they are comparing themselves to their White peers, who enjoy a completely different career experience, free from racism.

The impact of education on the Black workplace experience was a mixed bag for the respondents in my study. Many held professional qualifications and placed a high value on education but found that these qualifications did not lead to career progression at the same pace as their White peers. They felt that they were required to have more qualifications than their White peers to be considered for specific roles and some felt overqualified for the positions they held. Some of the Black professionals believed that education would help their careers, while others felt that having a high level of education was not fully recognised if they were Black. Many had no easy educational path and had to work part-time to fund their studies.

On the other hand, Black professionals without formal qualifications were made to feel inadequate and were treated differently in the workplace. This mistreatment resulted in a double bind for them, as having a qualification did not guarantee career progression while not having one resulted in adverse treatment. Participants felt that the value placed on their qualifications by organisations was less than in the case of their White peers, and therefore the return on their educational investment was lower.

These findings represent one of the many highlights of the systemic racial barriers faced by Black employees in the workplace – that even when they have high levels of education and qualifications, their qualifications are devalued.

Ethnically diverse employees in the UK workplace face challenges in their careers due to racism, and these challenges become even more significant at senior levels, reinforcing the view that the traditional approach of 'working hard' does not work for ethnically diverse employees.

There is a perceived lack of 'cultural fit' as they try to conform to the White organisational culture, leading to a two-tier employee experience where Black employees feel as though they are on the outside looking in at the different experiences enjoyed by their White peers. Black employees reported working harder than their White peers but without career support or guidance.

They felt that their hard work was not being valued and that they were seen as disposable resources. Additionally, the value placed on their education and qualifications was lower. These findings highlight the need for organisations to address and change their cultures.

Racial Discrimination

Many Black people in the UK feel held back in their careers due to racism. In my study, 87% of the interviewees (26 out of 30) felt excluded from fully participating in the workplace because of racial discrimination. The respondents described three dimensions of organisational culture that affected their careers: racial, cultural and organisational. They mostly had negative experiences in the workplace, where they felt marginalised, stereotyped and excluded. They described a primarily White dominant and hostile work culture, making them feel like outsiders and constantly on edge.

Black employees often felt forced to act a certain way to fit in and blend into a White organisational culture. They believed they could adopt aspects of Whiteness, but being a visible minority made it impossible to hide their differences completely. This complex phenomenon is known as code-switching. Code-switching involves adjusting one's style of speech, appearance, behaviour or expression to optimise the comfort of White people, particularly in professional settings (McCluney et al., 2019).

According to research conducted by the CIPD in 2019, nearly half of Black and ethnically diverse staff in the UK feel they need to hide their true personalities at work. The study, carried out by the consultancy Utopia before the COVID-19 pandemic and surveying 2,000 UK workers, found Black and ethnically diverse employees felt pressure to aspire to a particular expression of professionalism that favoured their White counterparts. As a result, 49% said they felt they had to mask part of their identity to fit in at the office, compared to 43% of White workers who said this.

Whilst the participants acknowledged social class as a barrier, they felt that racial discrimination was the main barrier to progression. They explained that, while White working-class colleagues could progress and become middle-class, Black employees would always be viewed as Black first and foremost and treated accordingly.

The professionals I spoke to referred to systemic and structural racism and felt they had to choose between keeping their heads down or risking the consequences of challenging discrimination. When they complained about racial discrimination, they often faced retaliation and resigned or were forced out of their roles. They also experienced undermining by line managers, colleagues and direct reports. They saw senior White managers getting away with extremely derogatory behaviour, including racism in the form of victimisation, bullying and harassment.

Having a supportive line manager was important for Black employees to survive in their job. Still, many found themselves in a precarious position because the line manager was often the perpetrator, or the line manager enabled the discrimination and took no steps to support them. Even where the direct line manager was not the perpetrator, respondents found that their line manager would not support them and, in some cases, the line manager participated in the victimisation, bullying and harassment through collusion.

This links in with the need for Black people to have a sponsor at work, someone who will advocate for you when you are not in the room. Participants expressed that, instead of acting as advocates, they experienced some White line managers throwing Black employees under the bus. This phenomenon led to institutional discrimination. The participants felt worn down and exhausted by discrimination and not seeing anyone internally who genuinely wanted to help.

Participants evidenced that, when they made a complaint of racial discrimination, they often commenced a slippery slope to the end of their careers. They described White managers and HR colluding against them in White solidarity to reframe and rationalise why an incident/situation had not occurred due to their race. One participant explained that, when they accused their line manager of racism, they were viewed as having attacked their line manager.

This then resulted in victim reversal, whereby the participant was deemed to have disrespected their line manager by accusing them of racism and subsequently found themselves in an untenable working environment with all senior management turning against them.

Participants provided harrowing examples of senior White managers 'getting away' with extremely derogatory behaviour, including racism in the form of victimisation, bullying and harassment. Roland described an incident where he had been working at director level and his line manager bullied him in front of senior colleagues and gave him responsibility for complex and challenging work beyond his remit. Colleagues spoke to him afterwards but did not say anything in the meeting. In this sense, racism is being experienced in a blatant form, not subtly. Eventually, Roland felt he had no choice but to leave and take a step back from his career. Complaining would have been of no use in his opinion, given the perpetrator was the chief executive.

In some organisations, the participants felt that their White peers had been groomed for senior roles and had a sense of entitlement and privilege. Participants spoke of knowing not to bother applying for certain positions as they were earmarked or, on some occasions, created for White candidates.

I have both witnessed and been personally affected by situations whereby line managers have planned restructures, relabelled jobs or removed responsibilities to give a White employee a job currently occupied by a Black person. These experiences created problematic environments for Black people to navigate.

Despite the negative experiences, some contributors used discriminatory experiences to motivate and mentor junior colleagues on avoiding pitfalls and found a sense of purpose in helping others navigate hostile environments. The responses from the participants showed that racial discrimination was a persistent issue in their careers, with a third considering or in the process of leaving their jobs due to the racial discrimination they faced.

When I spoke with Lemar, he quoted Toni Morrison (1975), saying that racism is a distraction that keeps Black employees from doing their work and continually explaining themselves. He described the complex web of racialised practices in UK institutions that are known and felt by Black employees every day, but are invisible to or accepted by the White majority who reinforce racist workplace cultures through ignorance or bias:

> *In the case of race and race equality, we are challenged by not just racist acts, but systemic racism in its practice, policies and procedures that prevent people like me, not as its aim, but as its by-product, is what happens in my experience.*

Even when identified as high-potential employees, Black professionals felt they were not given the same development opportunities as their White peers, who were promoted more quickly. This disparity led to participants feeling ignored and disheartened, and some even left their organisations to look for recognition elsewhere. Lemar described talent management and succession planning as 'hopelessly flawed' and said it often reflects the current management team and reproduces past biases. Because there is often no equality aspect to the process, racial prejudice is inevitable.

Only 7% of the Black professionals believed corporate development programmes aimed at ethnically diverse employees were positive for their career development, while 43% thought they had the potential to be positive if adequately designed. However, many participants felt that these programmes were performative and did not address the root cause of glacially slow career progression for Black employees, which was racial discrimination. Some Black professionals reported attending poorly executed ethnically diverse development programmes that harmed their careers, with no job opportunities at the end.

Participants expressed the view that, even if people had the intention to do the right thing, there was a reluctance to rock the boat and, whilst diversity and inclusion policies were a tool for change, policy development took too long to implement. The responses in relation to lived experience of organisational culture revealed hostile, White-dominated working cultures, where complaining about discrimination was often futile. Racial bullying, harassment and discrimination were a constant feature from all angles, including line managers, colleagues and direct reports.

The responses from the Black professionals showed that racial discrimination was a persistent issue in their careers. A third of the professionals had considered leaving or did leave their jobs due to racial discrimination they faced. They described discrimination in the form of racial harassment, sabotage, lack of promotion, unfair talent-management processes and more. The impact of discrimination was profound, causing ill-health, stress, anxiety and depression. Some participants had to retrain or accept more junior roles, while others became self-employed to avoid further discrimination.

Interviewees felt discrimination caused a loss of confidence and made it difficult to progress in their careers and that it was a driver of unemployment among Black professionals. They felt organisations accepted discrimination, and it was, therefore, institutional. Whiteness was viewed as a barrier to progression, meaning Black people were often undervalued in the workplace.

Types of Racial Discrimination Experienced

Sadly, all of the participants I spoke to had experienced racial discrimination at work and the fact that none of the respondents had escaped racism throughout their careers revealed the commonality and pervasive nature of racism in the Black experience. Participants experienced racism in all forms throughout their careers, including structural, systemic, institutional, modern-day racism and Whiteness. Black professionals opened up about the various ways they had been discriminated against and their frustration that racism had impeded their careers.

Interviewees described microaggressions and saw these as akin to continuous low-level daily attacks due to their ethnicity. This took the form of being labelled as aggressive, whereas similar behaviour from their White peers was viewed as assertive. There was a lack of acknowledgement for their work whilst others took credit. An example was given of raising a pertinent point in a meeting and being ignored, followed by a White colleague making the same point and being recognised and praised for their contribution. Participants described producing substantive proposals and senior White colleagues taking their ideas and receiving the credit.

Interviewees explained that, over time, this had a grave impact on their career as they did not receive credit for their work and were not seen as high performing. This contributed towards being overlooked for promotion. Participants observed White colleagues not engaging them in conversations, or informal chats in the lift or corridor, or being completely ignored. In my experience, microaggressions are often subtle; they can be one-on-one and often go unnoticed by others.

On other occasions, microaggressions are more blatant. Whether the microaggression was subtle or blatant, it was always met with complicit indifference by White colleagues in earshot who often saw it as trivial. When I spoke with Femi about this, he noted the following examples of microaggressions experienced at his current workplace whereby White colleagues made the following comments in front of other colleagues:

> *We knew [redacted participant name] was upset because he does 'that thing they do with their teeth'; 'you've done well for yourself – considering'; 'we are going to excuse you guys from certain parts of this process because we're talking about project management and a lot of it will probably go over your head'.*

This was despite Femi holding foundation and practitioner project management qualifications. Apart from being rude and disrespectful, these racist remarks were made in open fora and everyone present turned a blind eye. The ideas of bystanders and upstanders are central to understanding how people respond to injustice. A bystander is someone who witnesses harmful behaviour, such as bullying, harassment, or discrimination, but chooses not to intervene or offer support. In contrast, an upstander takes action to help those targeted or speaks out against what is wrong. In many situations, the presence of an upstander has the power to change the outcome and offer meaningful support to those affected. Respondents also referred to many examples of unequal pay in their base salaries and disparity in bonus payments and pay increases. They also described taking on additional responsibilities and having to spend many months and even years attempting to have their roles re-evaluated.

Participants explained that, when they discovered they were being paid less and raised it with their employer, there was never a satisfactory outcome. Line managers would attempt to justify the pay differential rather than address it. The pay was never rectified, and the participants normally ended up leaving the organisation. The Black professionals articulated that, even when they obtained senior positions, they were underpaid and female participants believed that intersectionality (being both Black and female) was an additional factor, as they felt that women were not as confident as men in applying for promotions and negotiating pay.

I spoke with Claudette who is a mid-career professional in the local government sector. She explained that unequal pay had been a constant feature of her career that she had been unable to address. Claudette stated:

> *I think there's always been a history of White counterparts ascending a lot quicker than an ethnically diverse employee. And they've always had higher roles, higher salaries. That's just the way things have always been. Things have changed but very slowly and very slightly. You do see some progression in some sectors but it's not at the same level, and I do think you have to almost prove yourself a lot more. It just takes a lot longer. Right now, a lot of my colleagues who are doing the same role as me, they're earning a lot more money than me.*

Claudette's description of needing to prove yourself more resonated with the concept of additional barriers to progression described earlier. Black employees felt that, in addition to individual discrimination, organisations had systems in place to restrict the progress of Black employees. Participants disclosed harsh treatment at board level where they were admonished in front of senior colleagues and singled out for unachievable performance targets. They felt that toxic cultures impacted unfairly on Black senior managers and left them exposed. Shaun told me that blatant discrimination was still occurring and that Black people were not supported in these situations. It felt that Black people were abandoned when they experienced racial discrimination. Shaun explained a situation he found himself in:

> *Where people get comfortable with you and they can make remarks or jokes which they certainly wouldn't make about others and you have to call them out on it.*

> *As an example: I was running sessions for a training programme for all staff along with other senior leaders. The CEO had been to see a number of them and one of the senior leaders suggested that there should be a little competition on feedback ratings and whoever got the best feedback ratings would get an extra day off. The Chief Executive piped up and says: 'No, no, no, there are two people [redacted names] who are by far the best at doing this sort of thing. And everybody knows, you know, the scruffy Black man with the dreads is gonna win.' Now he thought he was giving me a compliment on my delivery. He thought it was OK to make that joke because he knew me. He didn't describe the other person by their ethnicity or make a joke about their appearance. When he said that there was deadly silence on the call. Next to 50 people heard it. And what was amazing was only two people said something. He later called me personally and apologised.*

The issue of bystanders not intervening was a constant problem for Black employees; it sent a message that racism was tolerated or condoned. Participants observed and experienced that challenging discrimination destroyed Black employees' confidence and potentially their careers.

They explained that the aftermath of a devastating discrimination experience left them in a precarious situation where it was difficult to talk about what had happened to them. This was due to confidentiality clauses arising from non-disclosure agreements or because they felt ashamed of what had happened and wanted to put it behind them, believing that it would damage their career. This created additional trauma and contributed to the time it took for people to recover from their experiences. Clearly, these situations also held back their career progression.

In an attempt to be placed on a training course, Femi's line manager advised him to try and secure funding from HR, and stated:

> *Why don't you use the race card? – it seems to have helped your people with their careers.*

These types of comments are shockingly flippant and blatantly racist. Yet tackling these issues was problematic. There was the issue that, whilst in conflict with their employer, they still had the predicament of requiring a favourable reference to secure a new job. Participants referred to successful telephone interviews which were followed by unsuccessful face-to-face interviews, which they attributed to racial discrimination. Sharma told me that she was not accepted in her previous organisation due to racial discrimination and noted:

> *Yes [I have been discriminated against] in two organisations ... so if you're in a leadership role, people don't want anything other than the soft version of what they consider to be management ... I'd say once you start being strategic, managing large budgets, making real decisions, they find that that sticks in their throats if you're in a White ... dominated environment. They find it increasingly hard to take instruction from you and so what happened with me is they ganged up against me because they just thought they were better. Why would they want to take instruction*

> *from me or direction from me, particularly on strategy and budgets? I found staff that were reporting to me they ganged up with my boss. She [my manager] then devised a scheme where she thought I would be better off working in diversity, which I refused to move to. And then I found that the weight of the organisation came down against me, not because they didn't recognise that something wrong had happened, but because they don't want to admit to it.*

These situations rarely had positive outcomes and often led to the exit or ostracisation of ethnically diverse employees. This example demonstrates the collusion that occurs when racial discrimination is raised and the bizarre approach of moving ethnically diverse professionals into specialist diversity roles if they complain of racism. These organisations are essentially telling victims of racism to move into DEI and solve the problem for the organisation! – instead of dealing with the racist behaviour.

A female participant in the local government sector described leading on policy development and her line manager removing this responsibility and asking her to set up a diversity staff network instead, based purely on her colour. Other respondents reported that organisations that were particularly struggling to understand the role of diversity, equity and inclusion would frequently attempt to move Black professionals into equalities roles, even though they had no experience in the field. As well as being an inept practice, this approach could potentially damage the profession if it is viewed that being Black is the only criterion needed to carry out such work.

This section has examined the different types of discrimination faced by participants and the damaging effect this has on Black employees. The next section analyses the impact of racial discrimination.

Impact of Racial Discrimination

Thirty-three per cent of the participants considered giving up or gave up on their chosen careers due to experiencing racial discrimination. Twenty-seven per cent of participants decided to take a step back in their careers at some point due to the discrimination they had faced. These findings show that a third of participants considered giving up or did give up their careers or decided to take a step back due to racial discrimination. If one in three Black people in this sample were forced to take such drastic action, this is a worrying indictment of the treatment of ethnically diverse employees in the workplace.

It also demonstrates a damaging system where racial discrimination at work is costing ethnically diverse employees their livelihoods. Participants described discrimination in the form of racial harassment, sabotage, lack of promotion and unfair talent-management processes. They expressed the view that racial discrimination had derailed their careers and that the experience was traumatic and depressing.

Some participants decided to become self-employed rather than work for an organisation where they could potentially be a target for racial discrimination. Accordingly, some participants had given up on a broken system. Black professionals explained that another impact of discrimination was that they often needed to take some time away from work to rebuild their confidence, refresh their skills, connect with their networks and families, and regain focus.

They felt it was important to have positive people around them when they were going through these workplace challenges and preparing to relaunch their careers. They felt that the impact of racial discrimination caused ill-health and poor wellbeing and they experienced stress, anxiety and depression as a result. In this sense, ethnically diverse employees had a limit to the amount of racial discrimination they could bear, and it was important from a health and wellbeing perspective to recognise when one had reached this point.

I interviewed Donna, a senior executive working in a local authority, who felt that racial discrimination was rife and going unchecked in organisations. Donna shared that the experience of racial discrimination could be quite damaging and reflected that:

> *I think having had a really … traumatic experience of being systematically harassed and discriminated against in an organisation. I think that I decided no, I'm not doing this, I don't want to do this, and I don't want to put myself in this position ever again and I think that experience unfortunately is not uncommon … for me, what that's meant – wanting to retain independence, you know, to basically be able to market my skills and experience on my own terms, i.e. consultancy interim kind of work. That's a direct result of feeling that you just don't get the support and it's so easy to become a target. And I think this is manifestly racist. But yet all organisations won't recognise this … and I see it all the time. And I've also, in my role, been able to look at statistics which just show how much less successful*

> *[ethnically diverse] applicants ... are for progression, promotion and appointment. It is quite startling.*

When racial discrimination became unbearable, participants thought about retraining to work in different fields, such as nursing, teaching and foster care, or accepted more junior roles. This shows the depth of the impact of discrimination and the serious consequences of racism.

Black professionals referred to being left damaged by organisations and described their coping mechanisms to deal with structural and systemic racism which included escapism, external support networks and religion. Participants reflected that the impact of racial discrimination meant it was often difficult to continuously progress within the same organisation. The participants often had interrupted career histories, due to discrimination, which was difficult to explain to prospective employers and was met with harsh judgement from recruiting companies.

They voiced that discrimination caused them to seriously doubt themselves and wonder whether, as a Black employee, it was possible to excel in one's chosen career. Consequently, racial discrimination in their careers was a constant, exhausting battle. I met with Shaniah, a mid-career professional with a background in local authorities and the NHS. Shaniah had experienced racial discrimination and noticed the impact it had on her confidence when seeking future roles. Shaniah noted:

> *It affects your confidence to go for, you know, higher positions. I know it has affected my confidence definitely, because you start looking at yourself and wonder if you're good enough, you start wondering when you go there, you know, what you're going to face, you*

> *remember the times you've had those experiences and how it made you feel, or how it made me feel ... each job I was applying for ... one part of me is saying I don't think I want to work, I hope they don't call me to offer me the job, and another part of me wants the job because I need the money and I want to go back into work, so you get that bit going on and it's all because your confidence has been knocked down.*

The loss of confidence has a profound impact on the ability to bounce back and start again. Unfortunately, these racist incidents led to many examples of having to start over, which is draining and can cause employees to go backwards in their careers. This experience was shared by other participants who left their roles without another job to go to, meaning that racial discrimination was unfortunately a driver of unemployment amongst Black professionals.

However, the vast majority were not in the financial position to leave their role and therefore had to endure the discriminatory treatment. Black professionals initially hoped that their employers would resolve the issue so they could move on, but whilst raising their concerns, it became apparent that the discrimination was intentional and that the line manager would rather the individual left than address the discrimination.

Deliberate racial discrimination was raised by many of the participants and there was a feeling that organisations turned a blind eye to discrimination as it was deemed acceptable workplace practice. Black professionals felt that this view was reinforced by constantly only seeing White senior leaders around them.

They expressed the view that, whilst they were feeling demotivated, they were witnessing their White counterparts being extremely confident and supported in their roles. I spoke with Doreen, who is a mid-career professional working in the local government sector. Doreen felt that Black people were regularly underpaid and were often told to be grateful they had a job and so should not complain about unfair pay:

> *The first time I was discriminated against, in ... [redacted local authority], even though it was a defining moment, everybody knew that the two Black people who were doing the majority of the work were on the lowest grade. It was difficult because someone could turn around and say you got the opportunity, but we were actually not being paid correctly.*

This speaks to the notion that Black people often feel undervalued in the workplace despite working hard and being well-educated. Some of the Black professionals I spoke to felt that racial discrimination made them more determined to succeed, and they used their negative experience of discrimination to motivate and mentor junior colleagues. This provided them with a sense of purpose and helped them find positives in a negative situation. Participants also witnessed the negative treatment of other Black colleagues which raised their awareness of the racial context within which they were working. Talent management is discussed next.

Talent Management

Only 17% of the participants had been identified for formal succession planning. The Black professionals expressed the view that they were mainly identified for informal opportunities by a line manager, with only a very few being identified as part of corporate talent-management schemes. In effect, Black participants were excluded from succession planning which was largely an intervention reserved for White colleagues only. This leads to the question of whether anti-Blackness precludes certain employees from benefitting from organisational career-development resources.

The Black professionals I spoke to expressed the view that, even when they were identified as a high-potential employee, they were not developed further, whereas they felt that their White counterparts were subsequently developed and promoted. This experience left participants feeling overlooked and disheartened, and caused some to leave their organisations to seek recognition elsewhere.

Participants described the experience of working for a public service broadcaster and explained that talent management operated differently for their White counterparts who secured assignments and attractive project work, apparently without any selection process taking place. I have seen this approach in organisations, whereby talent schemes appear deliberately designed to exclude Black employees. Worryingly, participants' experience of succession planning has been that it is largely an avenue to secure promotions and opportunities for White colleagues and has not been a route available to them.

One participant, Shaun, had deep experience of shifting organisational cultures through robust strategies that explored systemic changes in policy and practice. Shaun explained the problem with talent management and succession from his perspective:

> *So, talent management and succession planning are one of those HR processes … which is hopelessly flawed, and by that, I mean there is no rigour or evidence applied to it. Most organisations use the nine-box grid, and it is a methodology which has been completely discredited in the research across Europe, which finds that it is just a driver for bias. Because in the worst cases, it's not pegged to any evidence. It's just a subjective view … And I've had that experience at other organisations where they've used the nine-box grid, and it only ends up in a direct reflection of the current management team.*

Here, Shaun was describing the effect of utilising talent and succession schemes that reproduce what has gone before. There is often no equality dimension to the process at all and therefore racial bias is an inevitable outcome. Ethnically diverse employees were largely excluded from succession planning and there was a lack of sponsorship and investment.

I asked respondents about the impact of mentors, sponsors and networks on their careers. When asked, 17% had experienced having a corporate sponsor at work and 25 out of 30 participants (83%) had experienced having a mentor. Of those who had benefitted from having a corporate sponsor at some point in their career, the sponsor was mainly their line manager, except for two participants where the sponsor was a member of the executive team. This shows the lack of deliberate rather than accidental investment in ethnically diverse employees' career development.

Most participants had not experienced having an organisational sponsor to speak up for them on their behalf, offer them project opportunities for exposure, or support them with promotion and development opportunities. Whilst this was the normative experience, Nigel, a senior executive in higher education, explained that he had benefitted from having a corporate sponsor and noted the profound difference it had made to his career:

> *I am actually experiencing what it's like for somebody senior to be your sponsor. So, I've been invited to a variety of … dinners with, you know, Tony and Cherie Blair … I've never experienced this before. This is fantastic. [My line manager] said to me, 'I want to expose you to all aspects of … management. I want to expose you to all aspects of the whole [organisational] life, so you have a full picture.' And that's been invaluable … I would say it's exposed me to those things which are not in any manual that I have read. I've been on a number of leadership courses, read lots of those leadership and management books, and that stuff so either I haven't seen, or I just didn't notice it. Or it just didn't resonate because I guess it's only by experiencing it then I see it because I see how he works.*

Whilst participants felt that sponsors would have been extremely beneficial to their careers, most participants had only benefitted from mentors they had sourced directly. Participants also spoke of the power of reciprocal mentoring; they felt that having mentors and coaches was important for career development and for staying current and relevant in their field of expertise. They found that mentors and coaches could help to navigate the political, organisational and relationship nuances at play, particularly at senior levels. Some participants described having good line managers who inadvertently acted as mentors by providing opportunities for exposure and stretch assignments.

In contrast, other participants conveyed that they had experienced or observed line managers being intent on holding ethnically diverse employees back and, in some cases, destroying their careers. Participants described the devastating impact of line managers who acted as saboteurs to their careers. This happened through not providing opportunities for advancement, unfair appraisals, being given unreasonable workloads, being discriminated against by racial bullying, harassment or contrived disciplinaries, being accused of poor performance management or being demoted.

Participants noted that networks operated as discrete inner circles to provide access and exposure to promotion opportunities for White employees and that it was difficult for ethnically diverse employees to join. Participants expressed the view that the networks were often exclusive, as they were designed to support White employees, which made it exhausting to attempt to access them; therefore, being told to 'network' or 'speak to certain colleagues' often proved ineffective.

Experience shows that it is difficult for Black employees to be invited into powerful networks as they are not wanted in what are seen as White spaces. Participants felt that nepotism and the old boys' network were still in existence in many workplace cultures, and they often only learned of influential gatherings after the event. Reflecting upon his NHS experience as a senior executive, Roland observed:

> *The inner circle works to an extent to favour people of a certain group. This is where the cultural interface*

also has an impact. So, there are certain things that certain groups of people will do that basically some of the 'Black and ethnically diverse' people would not do, due to culture. I will give you an example ... groups of people used to go on skiing holidays so from my cultural background that is unheard of ... Members of that group started to get those senior jobs like director or general manager for Medicine, Nursing or Pathology and, not surprisingly, these were people who all went skiing together. So, from my experience, sometimes those types of things whereby organisations could say it's just social interactions and it's open to everybody, but the reality is, it isn't and sometimes those symbolic things are seen as important and organisations have got to start exploring to understand why certain people of a certain social group seem to be doing much better in terms of getting jobs within the organisation. So that's one thing that I know that happens in lots of organisations and I've seen that experience for myself first hand. And organisations have got to wake up to things like that and start investigating what's going on and certainly when it comes to promotions and career development and internal vacancies.

The participants believed that organisations felt particularly threatened by intelligent progressive Black people, and that to progress, it was a case of 'who you know, not what you know'. However, on further exploration, it became clear that it was a case of 'who White people know, not what they know', as regardless of who Black people know, this was not usually beneficial to their career advancement.

Participants revealed that the lack of genuine senior positive and inspirational Black role models was woeful and that ethical Black leaders in senior positions were often treated so poorly that it was off-putting for up-and-coming Black professionals. In my experience, senior Black employees with ethical values have been openly subjected to racial bullying and harassment, whereby senior colleagues collude to sabotage them, and they are also subject to microaggressions.

Participants felt the lack of Black senior leaders also meant ethnically diverse employees were constantly judged against a standard that did not include them. There was a strong desire for up-and-coming talented ethnically diverse employees to have more routes to gaining exposure and opportunities.

So what does this all mean? Well, the findings demonstrated that, for Black employees, succession planning was unlikely to apply, they were unlikely to be viewed as top talent, excluded from powerful informal networks and unlikely to have a sponsor. Ethnically diverse employees were effectively shut off from these key career progression routes due to structural and systemic racism. Knowing this was the case, some organisations offered development programmes for ethnically diverse employees – in other words, a potential route to career progression. This will be discussed next.

Ethnically Diverse Development Programmes

In the heart of organisational change, a profound challenge persists. Bhopal (2020) astutely observes that programmes aimed at developing Black and ethnically diverse talent often operate within a framework dominated by White privilege and a normative culture of Whiteness. These initiatives frequently fail to address the entrenched structural and institutional racism that disadvantages these groups at every level. Moreover, they perpetuate the notion that increasing diversity is solely the responsibility of Black and ethnically diverse individuals, absolving White groups from any role in driving change.

From a critical race theory (CRT) perspective, Bhopal (2020) critiques the objectives and effectiveness of diversity programmes crafted by White senior managers. These leaders, with control over what is deemed appropriate knowledge, often design policies that hinder the advancement of Black and ethnically diverse employees to senior leadership roles (Bhopal, 2020). This approach fosters a deficit racial discourse, further marginalising the position of these employees.

To overcome these challenges, Black and ethnically diverse development programmes must be radically reimagined. They should place the needs of these employees at their core and involve them in the development process. Additionally, credible diversity and inclusion experts should be integral to these initiatives, and leaders must not only sponsor them but also understand the transformative impact they can have, as Bhopal (2020) advocates.

We will now analyse participants' knowledge and experience of such programmes. Just 7% of participants believed that development programmes for ethnically diverse employees were positive for career development while 43% of participants believed that ethnically diverse development programmes had the potential to be positive for career progression if designed properly.

However, participants felt that organisational culture needed to change, rather than the leadership skills of ethnically diverse employees. Participants felt that a common HR approach was to try and 'fix' ethnically diverse people through development programmes, instead of addressing racial discrimination as the root cause of slow progression. None of the participants who had attended a Black and ethnically diverse development programme had received a promotion and, notably, participants described experiences of poorly executed ethnically diverse development programmes, which ironically set them back in their careers.

Black professionals also pointed out that corporate development programmes and graduate intake schemes favoured White people, and that some ethnically diverse development programmes carried a stigma that further ostracised Black employees. The study found that attending Black and ethnically diverse development programmes can have a debilitating effect on careers if not adequately organised and expectations are unclear.

The deficit model refers to the assumption that individuals or groups lack certain skills, knowledge or qualities, which must be 'fixed' or improved for them to succeed. In other words, it is 'blaming the victim'. When management training is specifically targeted at Black staff, it can inadvertently reinforce this model by implying that Black employees are inherently less capable or prepared for leadership roles than their peers. Instead of addressing systemic barriers, such as bias, limited access to opportunities, and organisational culture, this approach focuses on perceived shortcomings within the individuals themselves.

This framing perpetuates stereotypes and overlooks the structural changes needed to create equitable environments, such as tackling discriminatory practices or ensuring fair representation in leadership pipelines. By focusing solely on individual training, such programmes fail to address the root causes of underrepresentation and inadvertently reinforce the narrative that Black staff are less equipped to succeed.

A small number of participants (13%) explained that they were identified and selected for a very senior and prestigious ethnically diverse executive leadership programme at a public service broadcaster. However, it quickly emerged that the actual programme was not well thought through and was destined to fail. The programme was designed using a deficit model which suggested that there was something wrong with the ethnically diverse individuals that the programme would fix.

Participants described being left in limbo in their careers after attending the programme. The programme was full-time for 15 months and participants had left successful careers to join after being selected from over 400 applicants and undergoing a lengthy selection process.

The participants explained that the programme was little more than a publicity stunt for the organisation, and they were actively blocked when they applied for internal roles when it ended. Lorraine had felt traumatised after working for a broadcaster and she reflected on the impact on her wellbeing:

> *Like the fact that I had to go for counselling and trying to get my confidence back up thinking I've forgotten everything I already knew about [my profession] the fact that I went on a programme that's supposed to boost your … like you were meant to be all confident about your leadership abilities and being driven into a certain direction and the fact that you end up going in a totally opposite direction that's ridiculous.*

Lorraine felt that the programme did the opposite of what it was supposed to do and that, rather than enhancing her career, it had stagnated it. Participants described the programme having had a significant impact on their careers, whereby some found themselves out of work and ignored by the organisation at the end of it.

Participants pointed out that corporate development programmes and graduate intake schemes were promoting a lot of White people. Whereas the ethnically diverse development programmes, as well as not resulting in promotion opportunities, also had a stigma attached to them, whereby participants were further ostracised by White colleagues who felt they had been singled out for special treatment.

In my experience, attending ethnically diverse development programmes can have a debilitating effect on employees' careers if not organised and designed properly and if expectations about what will happen at the end of the programme are not made clear.

Natalie works for a public sector broadcaster and struggled to progress her career. When I spoke with her about ethnically diverse development programmes, she felt deeply that these programmes were a diversion designed by organisations to be a tick-box exercise whilst not dealing with the real issue of racial discrimination. She felt the impact on employee experience is profound but going unaddressed. Natalie articulated that:

> *I feel like it's not the same [employee experience] and they know it's not the same, which is why they give us these … special 'ethnically diverse' leadership programmes. And, it's good in a way, but it's like why do we need special leadership programmes? Like, why can't we just*

> *progress in the same normal way that every White person progresses, we just need a special programme, like we need to be taught something extra that they don't … And, even the programme [public service broadcaster], the thing about it is … they do not want to be diverse. They know they have to be, so they're trying to appear to be, but it's not what they want and so that's why … it's never going to work. It's like pulling teeth. They just want to be able to tick the box … And if you want to give them real tangible things that they need to change, they're like 'No, look, that's not what you're here for. You're here to fulfil this purpose so stay within those lines. Don't try to actually instigate any kind of change, that's not what we're here to do, OK? Just do your leadership thing and then, you know, take it from there.'*

Natalie was articulating the performative nature of some ethnically diverse development programmes, which do not have the interests of ethnically diverse employees at heart but instead are concerned with presenting a good diversity image. Participants believed that deep-rooted racism manipulated the public into thinking that organisations were actively seeking to be diverse, whereas the diversity development schemes were largely a charade with no jobs at the end.

Sharma also had experience of working at the public service broadcaster and of participating in a development programme for Black and ethnically diverse employees. Reflecting on the programme, she noted:

> *They were all like superficial schemes that made you feel special for a period of time, but didn't actually give*

> *you any access to, you know, the real decision-making process or insert you into the system in any way. So, you were like in a parallel system the whole time. Whereas I think if you are a White man of privilege and that's what privilege is, you are like totally in the system you're totally mainstream from the word go. But what I think these schemes that I was selected for did was just kind of run me in a parallel system, which gave me a little bit of an insight but didn't insert me into the real kind of structures of developing my career. And again, when its time ended, and you haven't got a sponsor and you know you're sort of running parallel, you get an insight but you're not really getting your hands dirty. I mean I think what would have been much more helpful is if I'd had a sponsor who actually said I want you to, I don't know, go and edit this programme or I want you to run this project for me or something which you know that was tangible that I would then put on my CV as a proper outcome.*

The Black professionals' views on the impact of 'unconscious bias' training on their careers were mixed. Only one of the 30 thought 'unconscious bias' training would help career progression of Black employees, while 27% believed that proper training could aid progression of underrepresented groups. The respondents felt that unconscious bias training was valuable only if other mechanisms were in place to change the experiences faced by Black professionals in career progression.

Respondents expressed the view that unconscious bias training would be useful only if other mechanisms were in place to change the experiences faced by Black professionals in career progression. Participants revealed that unconscious bias training could give White people the legitimacy to hold racist views and help people to learn how to effectively suppress their views.

They believed the effectiveness of the training should be measured by whether attendees changed their behaviour after the training; however, they had not noticed any real improvement in diverse representation after many years and many cohorts of the training in various organisations. Participants felt the training was a quick fix for external scrutiny but did not lead to a genuine shift in culture and behaviour. They believed face-to-face anti-discrimination training would be a better approach to confronting biases.

Instead, Black professionals suggested people should be held to account for those views and real action taken to eliminate racism. Most participants thought that merely holding unconscious bias training programmes, which varied in quality, did not make any difference. They highlighted the numerous negative experiences of ethnically diverse professionals in the workplace as examples that unconscious bias training was not effective.

They also felt that change needed to be led by the chief executive and senior leadership teams and believed that senior managers within organisations were often the people who were reluctant to attend the training. Additionally, they felt that the effectiveness of the training should be measured by whether attendees did anything differently because of awareness. In this regard, they thought that it would be exceedingly difficult to see any organisational impact. I spoke with Michelle, a senior executive in the NHS, who reflected that:

> *I think programmes like unconscious bias ... like understanding race or discrimination, all it does is give you information ... increases your knowledge, and may help you to learn and may influence your attitude and behaviour, does it make a difference to someone's career? I don't know, they may be able to answer the questions better when they were going for an interview. But there has been research that says that unconscious bias training does not have the impact that one intends.*

Black professionals raised the issue that not all discrimination was unconscious and therefore a one- or two-hour training course could not possibly tackle those who consciously discriminated. They further pointed out that, once employees were trained, it was no longer unconscious bias, it was just bias, and once employers were aware of this bias, what was their duty? Participants felt it was the responsibility of the organisation to ensure that bias was not acted upon.

Participants expressed the view that these types of interventions were awareness-raising at best and felt that face-to-face anti-discrimination training would be a better approach to ensuring that biases were confronted. This could serve to provide choices about how to adopt an inclusive approach to leadership rather than the compliance training approach. They felt that discrimination needed to be called out and labelled as such, where people in positions of power were deliberately stopping ethnically diverse employees from progressing, or racially harassing or bullying them. The next section examines Whiteness.

Experiences of Whiteness

You will have heard the term Whiteness in the book a few times now, but what does it really mean? Whiteness is defined by its invisibility and its absence, by a set of norms and hierarchy related to White privilege (Garner, 2006). Whilst Whiteness is often invisible to White people who go through life unburdened by inferior treatment, it is visible to Black people whose presence is questioned and racialised at every turn (Mahoney, 1997). Morrison (1993) asserts that Whiteness exists to 'other' all those who are non-White. Roediger emphasises Whiteness as being akin to the amalgam of economic social and cultural capital (Paynter, 2001) by Europeans. Whiteness is also perceived as being the polar opposite of Blackness (Garner, 2006).

Whiteness is a culture of seeing the world through the lens of White comfort and expecting your life to be better than that of other ethnic groups. I have seen Whiteness in action where White customers are treated with hospitality and respect whereas Black customers are treated with disdain. I have witnessed this at hotels, airports and shops. In workplaces, Whiteness shows up in the culture and practices which reinforce behaviours that exclude and ostracise Black employees. This includes forming in-groups, not sharing information, setting Black employees up to fail, excluding Black employees from promotional opportunities and biased recruitment practices. Whiteness leads to all-White leadership teams where nobody notices the lack of diversity.

Afua Hirsch (2018) refers to Whiteness as being 'an identity that was invented in order to provide the superior identity to blackness's inferior one' and refers to the pernicious issue of Whiteness being both normalised and hidden from open discussion, whilst Akala (2018) indicates that people racialised as White are unable to process major shocks to the system of Whiteness as the predetermined superior race.

In the profound depths of human experience, Blackness is intricately woven into the fabric of historical and contemporary racialisation and oppression. As we reflect on the concept of Whiteness, it's essential to explore the meaning of Blackness.

Blackness is a multidimensional concept that extends beyond mere physical characteristics to encompass cultural, social and historical dimensions. It represents a shared identity shaped by the legacy of colonialism, slavery and systemic racism, which has historically marginalised Black communities while also fostering resilience and cultural innovation (Arday & Mirza, 2018).

Blackness serves as a lens through which individuals navigate and challenge societal structures, often confronting exclusionary practices in education, media and politics (Burke, 2018). Furthermore, it is a dynamic identity that resists monolithic definitions, embracing diverse experiences and expressions across the African diaspora (Lillis, 2003). By acknowledging these complexities, Blackness can be understood as both a site of struggle and a source of empowerment.

Recent scholarly discussions, particularly within the framework of Afropessimism, highlight the persistent dehumanisation and negation of Black existence within societal structures (Ajari, 2024). Emerging as a critical theory in Black Studies and Africana philosophy, Afropessimism critiques the enduring presence of anti-Blackness and questions whether White society can truly overcome its deeply ingrained fear of Black people (ResearchEd, 2023).

This perspective reveals that Blackness extends far beyond mere racial categorisation; it represents a condition that exposes the limitations of European thought and the gaps in its historical narratives (Ajari, 2024). These insights underscore the complex and multifaceted nature of Blackness, emphasising its crucial role in shaping modern identities and social relationships (Jung & Vargas, 2021).

Essentially, Blackness is not just a racial identity but a lived experience that reflects the broader societal dynamics of power and oppression. It's akin to a mirror that reveals the cracks in the foundations of societal structures, highlighting the ways in which historical narratives have been constructed to marginalise certain groups. By understanding Blackness in this way, we can begin to see how it challenges traditional notions of identity and forces us to confront the deep-seated biases that shape our world.

Returning to the concept of Whiteness, this phenomenon was explored with participants, and 87% (26 out of 30) believed that Whiteness was a barrier to their career progression. The high proportion of Black professionals deeming Whiteness to harm their career progression highlights the way people of colour are subjected to different layers of racial obstacles that are clearly visible to them but not to others.

Participants observed that Whiteness functioned on a muted form of communication where one does not ruffle any feathers with overt emotions but displays a fake modesty. Participants expressed the view that Whiteness captured a notion around an unexamined centre, with inequality manifesting itself in reinforcing negative stereotypes about Black people.

Responses revealed that Whiteness made it much harder for ethnically diverse employees to progress; some participants referred to subcategories such as White Irish people who they described as being White, but not fully accepted. Participants reflected that Irish and other marginalised White groups had supported them in their careers and given them opportunities to develop. They also felt that where recruitment panels and senior teams were all White, particularly in urban areas, this was not reflective of the population and resulted in a lack of opportunities for talented Black professionals.

Participants referenced the Windrush scandal – which we discussed in Chapter 1 – as an example of Black people being expected to keep decades' worth of records to prove their immigration status, whereas White people would not be expected to do so, and described Whiteness as a mix of arrogance, inconsistency and power. Participants felt that Whiteness operated with a level of unease around Black people, as there was a level of guilt and discomfort. I spoke with Jerome, who after many years in the public sector, had moved to a role in the private sector. Jerome noted:

> *Privilege equals calmness, relaxation, lack of danger and freedom to think. It's like flying, air travel, Whiteness is like business class and Blackness is like economy class ... you can get to the same destination, but trust me, you've had a harder time getting there ... And they have more perks, they have better food, more leg space, all of those things help them in organising a better life and a better career.*

Jerome was referring to the hassle-free existence White people are able to operate in as opposed to the multitude of discriminatory hurdles placed in front of Black people. Participants felt that Whiteness was a loaded term that described White people from England, parts of Europe or elsewhere, and could also refer to somebody in authority and power.

Participants expressed the view that Whiteness often meant the incumbents would have a global view about an organisation whereby the ability to access the world, to make decisions, and have the power that comes from a position of privilege was granted from birth. Black professionals articulated that a minority person could internalise inferiority because they were not often at the centre of decision-making.

Participants also believed that Whiteness operated based on White people holding most key positions in the organisation and acting as gatekeepers, particularly at board level. Participants described a distinct in/out group mentality, which they referred to as a club that operated based on informal socialising. They felt that this group would be largely middle-class and Russell Group educated and, as such, would largely exclude Black people. However, they also felt that White working-class people could at some point join Whiteness. When I spoke with Mary about Whiteness, she observed:

> *It's not just any White person... I think it's talking about people who are White and who are privileged. So, they've got ... they're probably middle-class, they've gone to a grammar school or a private school or some boarding school. They've got two cars in the, you know, in the driveway. They can go on two or three holidays every year. They've got a huge amount of disposable income ... You know, life just seems to fall neatly folded on their laps. That's what I consider*

> *to be Whiteness, so they talk correctly, they're in an in-circle. That's what I consider Whiteness to be. I wouldn't put your low-income council estate individual in that category.*

Mary thought that Whiteness was about the middle class; this is true, but it does also encompass all White people, regardless of class. Participants described the environment of predominantly White organisations as the atmosphere in which one must operate while never having any of the benefit of sharing that privilege or any of the confidence and comfort of trusting that your environment has your best interests at heart. One participant described the environment as akin to facing psychological warfare where ethnically diverse employees constantly doubt themselves and must keep reaffirming that they are competent, as they do not receive these messages from their employer.

Instead, there is a feeling that Black employees do not belong in these indomitable environments and that they must continuously operate at heightened performance levels whilst always remaining hypervigilant for a potential discriminatory act. I spoke with Anthony, who expressed the view that White people had an unwarranted and unspoken fear of him; he noted:

> *There's a level of guilt, there's a level of discomfort … almost your presence in these spaces is an accusation and that's quite a lot to carry … They feel threatened by me because I am a man and I'm a Black man.*

Participants indicated that Whiteness was related to skin-colour superiority, and the privilege it brought people

– leading to dominance in the workplace. Responses implied that people who exploited Whiteness were always protected by a system that worked in their favour. They described historical public sector institutions as being heavily steeped in Whiteness and observed that White people were often unaware of their privilege.

Participants expressed the view that Whiteness was to believe that you have a right to everything you want, and observed that it was also something nobody talked about, which made it the norm and invisible at the same time. They gave examples of being described as a Black person, whereas a White person would be described as a tall or short person. On the reverse side, participants felt that Black employees were made to feel invisible and of less value by being ignored and denied access to opportunities.

Participants noted that Whiteness meant that White people were extremely well invested in by being introduced to the right people, being invited to exclusive events, potentially having parents with the right connections, being sent on courses and trips, and running projects. Participants felt White people benefitted from lifelong investment whereas Black people, at best, had a poorly run ethnically diverse development programme, lasting 6 to 12 months, and were then dispensed with.

Participants believed that White employees were likely to be seen as a shining star and taken under somebody's wing for mentoring and development, whereas Black people had to fight for those senior opportunities, which were often only granted in the toughest of organisations that White candidates had rejected.

Participants believed that Whiteness allowed White employees to make mistakes and develop. They also expressed the view that, rooted in this, was having things presented in a way that is palatable to White employees, which included the way ethnically diverse issues were presented in dominant White cultures. Participants felt that Whiteness encompassed White fragility and anything that was viewed as different to that was perceived as a threat to the status quo, the balance of power, and to traditional ways of operating.

Participants expressed the view that their experience of Whiteness manifested in myriad ways, including stereotyping, not being culturally White enough, or not being from a middle-class background. Participants felt that White colleagues had a negative image of them, which meant that they would never fit in. However, participants felt that the impact of Whiteness could sometimes be so subtle that it was difficult to complain about, as many of the incidents were open to interpretation.

Participants were concerned that Whiteness in the work context focused on trying to change or improve ethnically diverse employees through development programmes, instead of compelling those who benefitted from White privilege to change their mindset. They felt that a change of mindset would enable senior White managers to acknowledge the skills, qualities and expertise possessed by Black and ethnically diverse employees.

Participants recalled experiences where the work environments made them feel excluded. Mary recalled an interview where she was asked whether she visited the gym and the pub and whether she had children, to assess if she would fit into the culture.

Black professionals described experiences of succeeding up to a certain level in their careers but then being blocked due to Whiteness. They recalled White colleagues believing

Black employees should not work at senior levels and being particularly aggrieved when Black employees held more senior positions than they did. Participants who had succeeded in gaining senior management roles felt those who enabled cultures of Whiteness actively sought to remove them from their senior roles.

Participants expressed the view that it was no longer appropriate for a roomful of well-meaning White people to decide what happens to Black people in the workplace. Black professionals felt that people of colour needed to be in decision-making spaces and reflected that to be White within the context of the corporate environment is to be normal, competent, and have no aspersions cast on you and the ability to enter an organisation and live and die by your own efforts or your own ability. I spoke with Natasha, a senior leader in the education field, who noted:

> *I think that what it's meant is that I've constantly had to prove myself. I think that … it's the mixture of Whiteness and also their own kind of discrimination or prejudice around race … which means that you are different, so therefore you have to prove that you are as good as us … Whiteness means that you don't have to prove it. It is acknowledged that it is. So, if a senior White person walks into a room, you know, you just presume that that person knows what they're doing. Whereas a senior Black person walks into a room, there's a kind of, hmm, why are they here?*

One male participant described being the only ethnically diverse person in a cohort that had arrived at a hotel to attend a prestigious residential leadership programme and being mistaken for a delivery driver by the receptionist. When in professional work settings, participants were regularly mistaken for security guards and cleaners and felt that this demonstrated the subtle ways in which Whiteness associated Black people with their perceived place in society. A look at the different experiences based on gender follows.

Differences in Lived Experiences at the Intersection of Gender

My research revealed that Black male employees were viewed as a threat by White men in the workplace. This meant that their experience was overshadowed by a fear of the meaning of their presence. Male participants also felt they did not follow the same rules as other employees and were more harshly judged and stereotyped in terms of hypervisibility. Black male participants were also subjected to more blatant forms of racism, including direct bullying, harassment and discrimination.

In contrast, the experience of racism for Black women appeared in the forms of microaggressions, selective incivilities and other forms of bullying, harassment and discrimination.

Black females recognised that they faced additional prejudice due to their gender and that the intersectionality of race, gender and class could lead to a poorer employee experience and resultant lack of career progression.

These important observations illustrate that, whilst all of the people I spoke to experienced racism of some kind, the type of racism and antecedents behind it were sometimes different and this therefore impacted career progression in different ways.

Summary

Race was foregrounded in the Black professionals' careers and a third of them considered giving up or took a step back from their careers due to racism experienced. Discrimination was a constant battle that made it difficult to progress and seemed to be accepted by organisations, in the sense that little action was taken to combat it. As well as microaggressions, blatant racial discrimination was also a feature. Whiteness was viewed as a barrier to progression and participants described the work environment as akin to engaging in psychological warfare.

Moreover, responses revealed lived experiences of being held back from career progression due to racism and cultural exclusion. Discrimination intensified at senior levels and 'playing the game' did not work for Black employees. There was a lack of cultural fit in attempting to conform to White organisational culture and structural barriers caused zigzag careers. There was a two-tier employee experience where participants were effectively on the outside, looking in at the different experience enjoyed by their White counterparts.

Black employees described working harder than their White peers, with no career support or guidance but just an expectation that they should work harder than everyone else. There was a sense that Black employees were seen as low-hanging fruit that could be dispensed with easily. There was less value placed on Black employees' educational attainment.

I found that similar experiences were being recalled in completely different industries, at different levels of people's careers, in various geographical locations. I was taken aback at how ingrained into the fabric of workplaces these terrible racialised experiences had become. Yet, without speaking to people, you would never know this was happening and is still happening in many organisations.

The lived experiences of Black employees help us to get to the meat of the matter. We now understand how the racism sausage is made in the workplace, with Black people the unfortunate lambs to the slaughter; leadership appears to be all sizzle and no steak, and this has a detrimental impact on the Black employee's ability to bring home the bacon – in peace.

Following from the links between race and career progression, the next chapter looks at the lived experience of the intersection between HR management and diversity and inclusion.

CHAPTER 4

HUMAN RESOURCES: HEROES OR HYPOCRITES?

Real integrity is doing the right thing, knowing that nobody's going to know whether you did it or not.

Oprah Winfrey

Introduction

Having worked in the HR field for over two decades and having seen various changes in the world of work, I've often thought of HR professionals as being at the vanguard of future working practices. It's why I enjoy my profession so much. HR professionals have the mandate to horizon scan and to prepare and source the workforce of the future. For me, equity and inclusion are at the heart of the journey. Ensuring all employees can thrive and achieve their full potential is of paramount importance. Yet, the participants I spoke with were telling me HR and equity and inclusion practices were part of the problem.

This section explores the lived experiences of Black employees in relation to their interactions with organisational

Human Resources, in terms of policy, practice and culture. The experiences of diversity, equity and inclusion practices will also be examined.

Using a co-constructed approach, I listened to the participants' views on potential solutions to career progression challenges. Co-construction refers to the epistemological position of constructivist grounded theory which endorses the researcher and participants' co-construction of knowledge, with the objective of formulating an interpretive illustration of participants' accounts (Charmaz, 2000).

Human Resources

Participants expressed the view that HR policies and procedures did little to support their career progression or to combat the discrimination they faced. Participants revealed that equity and inclusion teams were not effective in tackling their racialised experiences in the workplace. No participants felt that the career pathway was clear for Black employees, and most participants felt that the career pathway into senior roles was not applied equally in HR practice or policy, creating a lack of opportunity. Participants described constant blockages and barriers and the absence of effective HR management practice in relation to diversity and inclusion. Nigel noted:

> *Often, what happens particularly as a Black man in the organisation is that I don't play by the same rules as everyone else and they don't play by the same rules as I do. So, there is the sort of corporate stance and things that are shared around, you know, being a positive message around how you promote and do great things or a promotion. But in reality, we know that there are*

> *more informal ways people get into organisations and get promoted. There are those people who are hand-picked to be in positions because they're deemed to be available, suitable and the right people, but it's not transparent. It's not fair, it's not what the policy and the practice state. So yeah, it is obvious ... The rules don't apply equally to different groups of people.*

Nigel felt that he was excluded from the informal progression routes reserved for White people. Participants expressed the view that HR managers did not attempt to address the practices that stopped Black people from progressing. The participants articulated that, whilst HR policies could address the formal processes, a lot of recruitment decisions were taken informally. For example, Black professionals believed that HR policies were not being followed, as vacancies were being earmarked for White colleagues rather than following a fair and transparent selection process.

Participants conveyed the view that HR practitioners were ill-equipped to deal with modern-day racism and asserted that organisational policies were used as rhetoric only if they suited the aims of senior management. It was felt that nepotism prevailed and there was always a workaround to avoid fair processes. Instead, participants revealed that HR focused on formal practices, such as talent management and succession planning, which further excluded Black employees.

Participants observed that racially discriminatory experiences of Black employees were not tackled by HR managers and their involvement often made the situation worse. Some participants recalled making the difficult choice to leave organisations which they felt were operating racially discriminatory practices and to take different career paths. Nigel felt that the HR practices enabled Whiteness, noting:

> *The real rules are unwritten and unspoken. But they are known by the club ... And I would say, largely part of Whiteness is this feeling of eliteness and superiority. So, given that there is this underlying feeling that only other Whites are intelligent enough to be here. So, the door is open, in fact there's two doors, there's one door that fits five people, six people, eight people. That's the door for the Whites to come in and there's another door which is half a person wide, and it opens once every five years and that's the door for the non-Whites to come in. So, there are two doors, you can come in all 20 of you and whichever one of you manages to squeeze through that door once every five years you'll be in.*

Nigel was explaining the way HR practice manifests itself in organisations in relation to career opportunities for Black people. In his view, opportunities for people of colour are limited and tightly controlled. This speaks to the fear of having more than a couple of Black employees in senior roles, which is associated with White fragility. Participants expressed a view that career pathways into senior roles operated nefariously through networks and allies, rather than through formal HR policies and practice, often meaning ethnically diverse employees were forced to exist on the fringes of the organisation.

When seeking HR interventions to tackle these issues, participants found there was a lack of understanding and action. Participants noted the barriers for Black doctors and nurses seeking promotion in the NHS, having to job-hop to progress, and not being acknowledged for their ideas, but instead, having their ideas stolen. Participants saw this as an HR problem but did not feel HR could or would adequately address their concerns regarding discriminatory practices.

The role of HR was a constant theme in the racialised experiences of the respondents. Of the participants, 37% shared that they had been bullied or harassed at work and 47% had raised concerns regarding racial harassment or discrimination with HR practitioners. However, there was seldom a positive outcome and they were often forced out of their role. In relation to complaining to HR about discrimination, I spoke with Oba, who worked in a broadcasting organisation, who noted:

> *One time when I did speak – I didn't file a formal complaint about racism, but I did speak to HR ... a particular person subjected me to racism. HR did nothing about it and then the person was pretty much almost cocky to me the following day ... it wasn't taken seriously at all.*

Oba said that the problem with formally complaining about racism was that it depended on '(a) who you're complaining about, (b) who you're complaining to, and (c) the nature of the organisation you're complaining within at the same time'. This participant felt that making a complaint was damaging to employees' careers. Lorraine attempted to raise a concern with the Diversity and Inclusion team and noted:

> *He basically said he has a lot of things on his plate ... This is [the public service broadcaster's] whistle-blowing line. And, yeah, if I've got a grievance, I can talk to my manager ... it wasn't even like a matter like*

> *that. I wanted to speak to him about a policy, where the organisation stands, what the [organisation's] policy is on a certain issue, hence why I went to … diversity and inclusion … because, you know, the diversity policy is like supposed to be your bag. But he didn't know that that's what I was trying to speak to him about and he just made an assumption and gave me the whistle-blowing lines.*

This example shows that, whether complaints were raised with HR or the equity and inclusion team, which in this case was part of the HR team, the outcome was unsatisfactory. Some participants questioned whether the equity and inclusion function should report to HR or directly to the chief executive and put forward that HR practitioners did not actively seek to use diversity data to drive practice.

Some participants settled their disputes with their employers and left, rather than facing a difficult employment tribunal case for racial discrimination or victimisation. They felt that organisations sought to avoid conflict and that, once an employee was in conflict through raising a grievance, even if they were right and it was upheld, it was very unlikely they would be able to progress afterwards. This was especially the case if a management decision was being challenged. Some participants had been unfairly dismissed after raising concerns of racial discrimination or had witnessed this happening to other Black and ethnically diverse colleagues. Lorraine further noted her poor experience:

> *I must have written to [redacted] HR director … saying that this [diversity programme] is a joke and this*

> *is such a waste of time and then things did change. But I think that probably stopped me from ever getting a role ever at [public service broadcaster]. I guess you have principles and values again which you kind of live by and if you don't feel that they're being met, I don't think I can, and other people sit there and just not say anything ... But I think it definitely affected me there.*

Participants felt that they were largely facing employment issues that related to HR practice and people management. However, they did not receive support or resolution when concerns were raised; instead, it was often the case that raising a complaint was the beginning of the end of their roles in the organisation, and sometimes of their careers. Participants described White HR managers colluding with line managers in racial discrimination cases and in matters related to career progression.

In effect, HR practitioners were making the discrimination worse, as when a Black employee complained, the response from HR was often to make statements that questioned the intention behind racially discriminatory acts and to take the White perpetrator's side in how the case was handled. Fundamentally, there was a view that HR practitioners lacked understanding of microaggressions and selective incivilities; this resulted in HR practitioners questioning whether such incidents were discriminatory or not. There was a strong view from participants that White HR practitioners sought to hide or deny that racism was happening and would rather settle the matter through a non-disclosure agreement than challenge racist practices.

Participants recounted situations where employers fabricated stories of poor performance or conduct about them to force them out of their jobs, resulting in microsabotage. Aisha, a mid-career professional in local government, recalled being bullied out of her role and having to train her successor; attempts to resolve the issues with HR practitioners exacerbated the situation and a settlement was reached. Aisha noted:

> *It made me reflect. It made me look at going into the interim market just to explore and to take stock. And, I think, yes, it did impact on my career because I felt I had stagnated, but at the same time following my departure, I was able to take stock. And, of course, you worry financially. How am I going to cope? And yet at the same time, recognising sometimes opportunities and reward come in different ways and being a bit more philosophical about it.*

Participants expressed an overall sentiment that HR was concerned with demonstrating meritocracy through career progression, whereas it should be concerned with challenging the status quo and delivering transformational change, as Black employees were less likely to succeed on merit alone.

Claudette described a situation where she had applied for a senior role that was subsequently withdrawn prior to the interview stage. A colleague later disclosed that the role had been discussed at the pub and it was clear that Claudette was the top candidate. However, the staff that would have been line-managed by Claudette complained that they would resign if she was successfully appointed to the post and the role was therefore deleted. Another participant discovered they had been marked down in selection assessments for promotion due to their ethnicity.

These accounts have shown that poorly executed HR and people-management processes can result in discriminatory practices. Further, HR managers tended to lack understanding of or were complicit in structural, systemic and institutional racism within their organisations, according to the participants. HR professionals often turned a blind eye to discrimination and exacerbated discriminatory practices in the workplace.

In considering the ethical obligations of HR professionals, it is important to acknowledge the practical challenges and potential repercussions they may face in the workplace. HR practitioners often find themselves in precarious positions where voicing concerns or deviating from instructions could jeopardise their job security, erode trust within the organisation, or adversely affect their performance evaluations and financial incentives.

These very real considerations can create a tension between ethical ideals and pragmatic self-preservation, potentially influencing decision-making processes and actions taken by HR professionals in their roles. The delicate balance between upholding ethical standards and navigating the complex realities of organisational dynamics presents a significant challenge that must be carefully weighed in any discussion of HR ethics and practices.

Diversity, Equity and Inclusion Processes in the Workplace

Only 3% of the participants believed that organisational approaches to DEI were fit for purpose and only 17% of the participants believed that organisational DEI approaches even had the potential to be fit for purpose. Participants felt that organisational DEI strategies were inadequate and accompanied by inexperienced and ineffective HR approaches, which inevitably led to poor outcomes.

They expressed the view that Black employees were underrepresented at senior levels and overrepresented at junior levels in their organisations. Many participants believed that DEI policy was merely a tick-box exercise and that it was difficult to raise issues of discrimination without being marginalised further or being forced out of the organisation.

Participants described Black employees receiving harsher and more punitive treatment during disciplinary processes and reiterated that the cumulative effect often resulted in them having to leave their organisations to seek promotion. Natalie spoke about her experiences with a diversity and inclusion team in a broadcast setting and noted:

> *I don't even go to them because it's a waste of my time. It's a waste of your time and you can say something in there, like for example, when I was – I went to the diversity meeting and I talked about the fact that the Black and Asian shows don't have regular producers and you could have heard a pin drop, like everybody lost it. And, you know, they were all scrambling. 'We're going to talk about this. We're going to address this. We're going to do this.' Because in that time, it doesn't look good for them ... Because they were in a diversity meeting and talking about how great they are and then you expose this and they're all, you know, scrambling.*

Natalie was describing the lack of progress on DEI in the organisation and the fact that some people had simply given up on expecting the racialised nature of the culture to change. This observation reinforced that Black employees can see through performative equity and inclusion and it is not in the organisation's interest to pay lip service where employees' lives are being impacted by the devastating effects of workplace racism and discrimination.

Shaun spoke about the need to boost the equity and inclusion profession. This participant described carrying out a detailed equality analysis for an organisation and the information being categorised as legally privileged and no action being taken with regard to the findings. Being an equity and inclusion specialist, Shaun felt that most equity and inclusion specialists did not have the expertise to lead cultural change and that most simply ran events rather than addressing important issues such as fair evaluation, diverse leadership or recruitment processes.

Participants expressed the view that equity and inclusion leads did not have much influence and were focused on the wrong things. Oba felt that equity and inclusion were not effective and noted:

> *I don't see equality and inclusion as effective most of the time and at best of the times, it's a rather confused function. It's not really well thought through. It's very difficult because what you're asking a professional to do is to find the solutions to hundreds of years of discrimination of adverse beliefs about certain subsets of people, of supremacy and beliefs too, so you ask that person to find solutions to those problems within the confines of the corporate structure and also to apply*

them and make sure it's understood. The reality of the matter is that those people normally don't – those people working on diversity normally don't have any power to even do that.

Participants felt that there was a powerful coalition within the equity and inclusion and leadership space that actively sought to undermine racial equality as an agenda item. There was a view that LGBTQ+, disability, and gender were the dominant areas of focus in terms of protected characteristics, and that when an issue of race was raised within their organisations, it was ignored. This resonates with my experience of leadership teams constantly asking HR and equity and inclusion to focus on other diversity areas despite the data and employees advising that there were serious discrimination and underrepresentation issues based on ethnicity.

Black professionals shared the view that HR managers were ill-equipped to handle racial discrimination issues and had not attempted to address informal practices that prohibited Black employees from progressing in their careers. HR practitioners' knowledge of equity and inclusion was found to be lacking and this exacerbated the situation. Respondents indicated that HR did not take racial complaints seriously. Most participants felt that equity and inclusion approaches were ineffective. Overall, HR and equity and inclusion practitioners had not addressed the underrepresentation of senior ethnically diverse employees but had contributed to making the situation worse. The next section looks at potential solutions to career progression challenges.

Co-Constructed Solutions

The final core theme of my research explored career progression solutions. Whilst a co-construction approach was deployed, I was careful not to present solutions to participants but instead asked open questions and allowed participants to convey their views uninterrupted before engaging in conversation. Participants put forward a range of recommendations to address the knotty issue of poor career progression outcomes for Black employees.

Organisational Development Solutions

How can organisations reimagine inclusive organisational development? According to Miller (2020a), in the pursuit of racial equality, leadership must embody activism, courage and inclusivity. As Miller (2020a:19) emphasises, White leaders must challenge racial inequality within their institutions, advocating for policy changes to prevent its trivialisation or normalisation. This call is echoed by Uwagba (2020), who advocates for 'White allyship' that involves self-sacrifice and addresses ethnicity pay gaps and other injustices.

Modern organisational development strategies advocate for an anti-racist approach. Miller (2020b:7–8) suggests that school leaders should confidently discuss race, adapt to demographic changes, cater to diverse learning needs, combat discrimination in staffing and foster inclusive institutional processes. Building on this, McCluney et al. (2020:52) propose three anti-racist models: proactive self-education on racism, embracing discomfort in acknowledging racist mistakes, and changing structures that perpetuate White supremacy.

Ozturk and Berber (2020:19) highlight the need to address organisational power hierarchies and subtle forms of racism, such as selective incivility. They recommend critical reflective training, increased Black and ethnically diverse representation, and amplifying Black and ethnically diverse voices. The concept of 'racial battle fatigue' (Smith et al., 2007:555) underscores the psychological toll of racial microaggressions, prompting some organisations to introduce Black and ethnically diverse wellbeing roles.

Scholars argue that a 'not racist' stance can be a form of racist violence (Lentin, 2018:5), and Kendi (2019) emphasises the importance of persistent learning and creating equitable structures. Kramer (2020) suggests ten pledges for advancing racial equality. Ben et al. (2020:206) outline four key areas for effective anti-racism: intergroup contact, training and education, communications and media campaigns, and organisational development. While diversity training can reduce prejudice, it must be well thought through to guard against unintended consequences (Ben et al., 2020).

Critical race scholars highlight the limitations of diversity management, emphasising how societal racial discourse can obstruct initiatives (Romani et al., 2019). Mungin and Stock (2020:1) stress that genuine commitment to anti-racism involves changing systems and structures, requiring leaders to couple solidarity statements with tangible actions.

Ultimately, becoming an anti-racist organisation demands sustained effort and commitment to dismantle entrenched inequalities. Leaders must prioritise tangible action steps and goals to achieve racial equity, ensuring that their solidarity statements are backed by meaningful change (Mungin & Stock, 2020:1).

Against this backdrop, participants indicated, overall, that organisations and the systems within them were racially discriminatory and required urgent change. From this standpoint, activism emerged as a conceptual approach to organisational development whereby participants indicated that active anti-racism, active understanding of the lived experience, active acknowledgement of the existence of Whiteness, and active allyship would represent a move in the right direction.

Consequently, participants observed that organisations first needed to acknowledge racialised practices and experiences in order to progress anti-racism and saw this as the first step towards a holistic anti-racist approach. This dilemma is a long-standing one, as raising Whiteness and activist allyship can be viewed as taboo and controversial in some organisations.

Participants indicated that public sector organisations had a duty to measure and embed progressive culture change that resulted in all staff feeling as if they belonged and could succeed. Sadly, some participants felt that the leadership within some organisations was so culturally entrenched in racism and disregard for Black employees that they were unlikely to see any positive change in their lifetime.

The sense of despair was palpable; however, I reflected that there is renewed hope in the wake of organisational responses to the Black Lives Matter protests and the change of UK government. Participants indicated that there was, generally, a lack of external scrutiny into the way ethnically diverse employees were treated in the workplace and that management teams with no racial diversity should be challenged.

Participants believed that leaders should have a fundamental understanding of the case for equality and then become active anti-racist advocates, including understanding their own biases and preferences and facilitating equity and inclusion at all levels.

Interviewees expressed the view that it was the chief executive's responsibility to ensure that there is a zero-tolerance approach to racism. This included not turning a blind eye to discrimination even if the perpetrator was someone in the CEO's inner circle, which would send a message across the organisation that discrimination would not be tolerated.

Participants indicated that structural racism created barriers to career progression for Black employees in a number of ways, including how policies were applied, how organisational practices led to different experiences and the type and distribution of work people were assigned to, and that this ultimately led to limiting effects on career progression. To tackle this, participants said that organisational inquiry was needed to understand the impact in different organisations with appropriate recommendations and action.

Interviewees highlighted that the impact of Whiteness on career progression was profound and should be tackled through comprehensive reviews of practices and training. Participants felt that even discussing race at work often caused problems and that it was an uncomfortable conversation for White colleagues. Examples were given of White employees being offended for being referred to as White people, whereas descriptive terminology to describe Black people went unchallenged. Some participants did not like the term 'BAME' and preferred Black people or people of colour.

Participants thought that the discomfort White people have when talking about race is a barrier to appropriately tackling the problem. Therefore, participants contended that organisational development interventions were required to talk about race and ethnicity. I was able to identify with racial discrimination avoidance as a potential obfuscation approach which resulted in nothing happening to tackle racism in organisations.

Interviewees indicated that, due to the exhaustion faced by Black employees in tackling discrimination at work, wellbeing should be a key consideration. Participants expressed the view that, given many ethnically diverse employees left organisations due to racism, exit surveys and interviews should seek to capture these data.

Further, participants indicated that culturally exclusive activities, such as doing organisational business in the pub, which was likely to exclude many people, should be thought through and alternatives such as lunch or coffee catch-ups would be more inclusive. In my experience, the exclusivity of these informal activities is often met with denial or is played down, and therefore making them transparent is a central issue.

We will delve further into solutions in the next two chapters. Role models and sponsorship are discussed next.

Role Models and Sponsorship Solutions

When asked about what would make a difference to career progression, 83% of participants believed that there should be more Black role models in senior positions. Participants conveyed that the paucity of Black leadership needed to be addressed and that, whilst there was a handful of Black leaders in some organisations, it was noted that there was significant and widespread underrepresentation. Participants expressed the view that public sector organisations should actively appoint ethnically diverse leaders to reflect the populations they served.

Whilst participants conveyed the need to see more ethnically diverse employees in senior positions, they drew an important distinction in wanting to see Black leaders who would be positive advocates. I spoke with Patricia who felt strongly that hiring more ethnically diverse employees into senior management positions could create positive opportunities. Patricia noted:

> *I think organisations need to get more Black people into senior management positions, everybody says that, yeah, tick. But ones that don't forget … OK! Get more Black people into senior management positions, but the ones that truly want to bring other Black people along with them … just think, OK, how can I help others? I'm not saying do shortcuts, you know, put everything in place correctly, but get more Black people in senior management positions, that understand some of the things that people are going through because we've all got stories to tell and I think there's a richness there if we can get more Black people into real senior positions … I mean like chief execs of organisations and, you know, directors of financing, HR, that really understand who they are and are willing to bring people along and truly believe in wanting to enhance and promote other Black people … I really believe it. And be accountable as well.*

Participants referenced the high number of Black role models in America and the positive impact this had on inspiring others to know that they had a genuine chance of success. Participants suggested that successful Black leaders should become sponsors and non-executive directors to represent and support vulnerable Black professionals who were facing difficulties.

Interviewees reflected on the way they had seen senior ethnically diverse employees treated in the past and found this to be off-putting and indicated that organisations had a duty of care not to bully, harass and discriminate against the few Black leaders that achieved senior positions, as this sent a very poor signal to other employees. In my experience, the optics of the poor treatment of senior Black leaders in some organisations, whilst shocking, has become normalised.

Thirty per cent of the participants viewed access to networks as important. Participants articulated that sponsorship could be a solution to career progression for ethnically diverse employees, if organisations based this on addressing underrepresentation and potential. They also expressed the view that people of colour needed to be given a voice to enable them to thrive.

Participants felt that ethnically diverse employees would benefit from genuine succession planning, reward, recognition and sponsorship. Black professionals indicated that sponsorship and mentoring should be purposeful rather than accidental and should be met with genuine levels of investment appropriate to addressing underrepresentation. Lemar noted:

> *There needs to be … formalised targeted sponsorship, it's been … kept a secret for too long. We need to get senior leaders in organisations to target sponsorship for underrepresented groups and, in this case, we're talking about Black individuals in the organisation. Sponsor them, use whatever method you want to identify them – that might be alumni of your development programmes … and sponsor them, adapt if you will a variation of the guaranteed interviewing scheme that was introduced for people with a disability that use that intervention, this is getting close to Rooney Rule-type positive action now, but use that tool, that device to ensure that you have more 'ethnically diverse' candidates interviewed and more ethnically diverse recruitment panels.*

Participants reflected on how Black and ethnically diverse employees should have more and better opportunities, such as secondments, placements and shadowing, where they were able to spend time with the chief executive or Chair of the board. Participants indicated that reciprocal mentoring could help ethnically diverse employees learn how to influence upwards and that Black mentors could share their career journey experiences to learn how to navigate racialised environments.

Respondents reflected on how it had taken them many more years to advance their careers than their White counterparts and therefore they wanted the pace of career progression for ethnically diverse employees to be monitored, including the application of selection criteria. It was felt that this would support leadership teams to be more reflective of the population.

Participants articulated a need for far more focus and concerted efforts on building networks of Black and ethnically diverse professionals at various levels to supplement the lack of Black role models. They felt that huge amounts of work needed to be put in to develop Black talent pools across all sectors. They believed that this type of network would help to put opportunities forward and minimise mainstream selection processes that screen out large numbers of Black candidates.

The next section looks at succession planning, recruitment and promotion.

Succession Planning, Recruitment and Promotion Solutions

Fifty-three per cent of the participants believed that improvements in recruitment selection and promotion processes needed to be made to eliminate bias, particularly through diverse selection panels. Participants were of the view that racially diverse recruitment selection and promotion panels should be mandatory and that, in the absence of internal senior ethnically diverse professionals, organisations should invite external ethnically diverse professionals to participate in these processes.

Responses indicated that diverse panels should review and scrutinise recruitment outcomes and decisions, as this would help to disrupt the system with an equality bias.

Participants expressed the view that competency-based interviews would help reduce bias and thought there was a need to actively monitor inputs and outputs from recruitment, career development, succession planning and talent management. It was further acknowledged that blind CVs would not prevent discrimination at the face-to-face interview stage.

Participants expressed the view that organisations should apply a guaranteed interview scheme similar to the 'Rooney Rule' for ethnically diverse candidates, where shortlists must include a diverse candidate, and review the rate of progress of Black and ethnically diverse candidates at each stage of the recruitment process.

Interviewees believed that organisations should recruit based on social values aligned to equity and inclusion and that this should be tested properly. Participants proposed that, for organisations to move towards a meaningful approach to racial inclusion, they needed to embed the values into culture and behaviours across the workforce. Participants advocated for transparent recruitment practices that moved away from informal nepotism approaches and towards fairness and transparency.

Participants expressed the view that talent management should entail coaching and access to senior leaders and should not only be linked to those identified as top performers, as discrimination will have crept into those processes and simply reproduce what has gone before. Succession planning and talent management needed to be tested for bias, and participation should not be the exclusive preserve of White employees. Participants conveyed that organisations delivering ethnically diverse development programmes must ensure they are designed properly with input from Black and ethnically diverse equity and inclusion specialists and have clear outcomes.

Further, participants felt that, once organisations had addressed the lack of progression of ethnically diverse employees through succession planning, sponsorship and development of effective anti-racist approaches that eliminated the progression gap, ethnically diverse programmes should be replaced with tailored development.

They highlighted that appraisal ratings should be reviewed to ascertain the fair application of scores and subsequent promotional opportunities. Participants further articulated that line managers should be held to account regarding the progression and retention of ethnically diverse employees, linked to ensuring managers have diverse teams.

Human Resource Management Solutions

Participants felt that ethnically diverse employees should be treated with respect and supported to achieve fair outcomes. They highlighted that it was too easy for ethnically diverse employees to be targeted by racist colleagues who were safe in the knowledge that they would get away with it. Participants indicated that complaints from ethnically diverse employees needed to be handled appropriately by HR and management and that there should be appropriate outcomes for race-centred cases.

Interviewees felt that HR personnel should have expertise in dealing with racial discrimination in the workplace and that raising a racial discrimination complaint should not be the beginning of the end of a Black employee's career. In my experience, HR staff can lack basic knowledge of what constitutes racial discrimination and have not sought to develop expertise before embarking on complex cases.

Participants highlighted that HR approaches were a major problem in addressing racial disparities in career progression. Participants expressed the view that HR staff were ill-equipped to provide appropriate interventions to address racially biased approaches to career progression within organisations. Biased performance appraisals fed into the problem, along with a lack of HR oversight of diversity data.

Participants noted that current HR interventions had the impact of continuing the discrimination and the lack of diversity and a lack of inclusion expertise compounded the problem. Participants indicated that HR staff needed to gain expertise in structural, systemic, institutional and modern-day racism and Whiteness.

Modern-day racism, such as microaggressions which fly under the radar of formal policy, was found to be a significant issue. The role of HR in addressing microaggressions was found to be critical, including the need for HR staff training and anti-discrimination policy reviews. To address the perpetrators of racist acts, participants expressed the view that anti-racism training should be provided and that diversity and inclusion outcomes should be linked to objectives.

Participants asserted that HR practitioner roles in race-centred cases needed to be reviewed and the lack of expertise in equity and inclusion had to be addressed urgently. HR required training in modern-day racism and the ways in which informal practices in promotion and selection were discriminatory.

Participants indicated that HR needed to move away from an approach which extols the myth that Black people need to be fixed through ethnically diverse development programmes and instead focus on addressing structural, systemic, modern, institutional racism and Whiteness to challenge discriminatory cultures. In so doing, HR had a responsibility to clearly articulate gaps in organisational policy and procedures that have led to gaping disparities and avoid cultural exclusion of Black employees.

Participants said that HR had a key role to play in moving from passive enablers of racial discrimination to an actively anti-racist approach that challenged key practices which reproduced bias. Diversity, equity and inclusion approaches are discussed next.

Diversity, Equity, Belonging and Inclusion Interventions

Fifty per cent of the participants believed that equity and inclusion approaches that secured cultural and systemic change would make a difference to the career progression and lived experience of ethnically diverse employees. Participants also expressed the view that credible diversity and inclusion specialists were those who could lead on thought leadership, insights, timely and creative solutions, tracking and monitoring key data trends, in addition to having passion and enthusiasm.

Black professionals indicated that many corporate equity and inclusion approaches were tokenistic and performative and that ethnically diverse representation up to board and executive level was required. Participants believed public sector organisations should ensure inclusive practices and be challenged by the government if their board is entirely White. They suggested co-opting external Black experts on to boards lacking racial diversity.

The diversity, equity and inclusion backlash referred to in Chapter 1 is interesting as it has uncovered tokenistic and performative practices. Black employees have long suspected that some organisations' approach to inclusion was not genuine, and recent events have only served to confirm this. Some disingenuous organisations recruit senior ethnically diverse leaders and then set them up to fail by not attempting to address cultures of Whiteness and anti-Blackness.

When ethnically diverse leaders come to the realisation that they are merely 'token' hires, the experience can be nothing short of devastating. It often leads to experiences of imposter syndrome, exclusion, marginalisation, bullying, sabotage and outright hostility. The inevitable impact on their performance is profound. How can anyone thrive in such a toxic environment, where the very essence of their being is eroded? If they must stay in these environments, they are often mentally drained and broken shadows of their former selves.

Consequently, some of these Black leaders decide not to linger in such hostile settings, choosing instead to safeguard both their careers and mental wellbeing. For Black professionals, the daunting task of evaluating whether a new workplace will be 'safe' – culturally, emotionally and mentally – becomes a critical challenge. This assessment is particularly difficult to make from the outside, leaving many to navigate uncertain waters.

Respondents revealed examples of working for forward-looking organisations that had integrated equity and inclusion into their structures and practices. This included competent, well-trained equity and inclusion leads reporting into the executive team, designing services from an inclusion perspective, and inclusion-based leadership evaluation and selection practices. Active allyship was required but was rarely a feature of the lived experiences described. Lemar described himself as a tempered radical and noted:

> *Tempered radicals are individuals who, either by choice or otherwise, find themselves at the fault lines of organisations and they try and fix it – right. So, they try and fix the faults within organisations and that's what I now know about myself and the organisation. That's what I try and do, it's a very hazardous job because you can, you know if you have a really bad week you can be perceived as a troublemaker. But that's not what you are. You love the organisation and you're trying to make the organisation better … it's also caused me to pick up the mantle and amplify the voice of the underrepresented … And at times, very much I'm putting my career, my personal career, on the back burner and representing others, whether it be in tribunal cases or internal grievances. And you know, really flying the flag for those who find it difficult, if not impossible, to represent themselves.*

Tempered radicals can form part of the solution, but due to the personal nature of adopting this approach, it may not work in all settings. Participants observed that many organisations were reluctant to set targets for numbers of ethnically diverse employees in leadership positions in the same way that targets were set for gender, and felt this would be a tangible step in the right direction and would distinguish employers that were willing to be held to account.

Participants also conveyed that organisational inclusivity accreditation was an important message to employees and prospective candidates and that evidence-based equity and inclusion data that tracks processes and identifies barriers is crucial to tackling underrepresentation of ethnically diverse employees.

They also felt that policies and procedures should be aligned towards complete inclusion and that annual equalities reports should be produced and scrutinised and challenged if there was no improvement. Participants expressed a need for racial diversity and inclusion to be monitored externally by Black equity and inclusion specialists, like the former Equal Opportunities Commission, to advise and consult on practices, policies and systems. This would enable organisations to identify gaps, subliminal messaging and institutionally embedded cultures.

Summary of Potential Solutions

Clearly, participants were not impressed with their interactions with HR and equity and inclusion teams in their times of need. As HR professionals, we often think about 'moments that matter' in employees' careers and when employees are in conflict, such as when they raise concerns of racism; this is a moment when HR and equity and inclusion professionals need to enact appropriate interventions.

Scrutiny of the treatment of ethnically diverse employees was needed as participants had experienced hostile cultures manifested in disregard, born out of anti-Blackness. Participants expressed the view that the CEO was responsible for equity and inclusion and that all leaders should be active anti-racism advocates.

Organisations should review the way structural racism and microaggressions impacts upon the career progression and employee experience of Black and ethnically diverse employees. Participants conveyed that where Black employees were in senior positions, organisations should have a duty of care to ensure they are not bullied, harassed or discriminated against.

Participants suggested tracking the career progression of ethnically diverse employees and reviewing succession planning to eliminate bias. It was also found that sponsorship and mentoring should be purposeful. Underrepresentation from board level down was a priority area. They further conveyed that positive discrimination should be considered along with targets for numbers of Black senior staff and accreditation.

HR practitioners were viewed as exacerbating discriminatory practices and needing equity and inclusion expertise to enable an effective review of HR interventions. Participants observed that equity and inclusion teams should adopt an organisational development approach. The co-constructed solutions illuminated the participants' desire for organisations to engage in an active anti-racist approach that centred on the lived experiences of Black employees, starting with acknowledgement of the existence of racial bias.

After learning of these interactions with HR and equity and inclusion professionals, I felt disappointed. So much change is needed, and yet these issues do not seem to be a high enough priority for organisations. It is clear to me that leadership is key – strong ethical leaders who see equity and inclusion as a crucial component for success.

However, the half-baked HR interventions and weak equity and inclusion described was problematic; in fact, it was a recipe for racism disaster. The treatment people of colour received after raising concerns merely rubbed salt in the wounds and left a sour taste in the mouth, to say the least. The next chapter explores the road to resilience.

CHAPTER 5

THE ROAD TO RESILIENCE

Never be limited by other people's limited imaginations.

Dr Mae Jemison

Reflections

I encountered many Black employees who gracefully shared the experiences of their racialised career progression journeys; in addition, my own complex experiences of career progression inspired the topic of research. It's heart-wrenching to know that doing a good or even a great job will not suffice; there are a myriad of barriers and hurdles that come with being Black in the UK workplace.

You must worry about being discriminated against; being sidelined; being set up to fail; being ostracised; being bullied; being sacked; being dehumanised; being used … I could go on and on. My husband Phil uses the phrase that people of colour often end up being either a token or a target at work. Who wants to be either? No one.

Black colleagues explained that, when they raised complaints of racial discrimination or bias, they were ostracised and forced out of the organisation. Those who stayed in organisations often remained at the same level for many years. I encountered several Black professionals who disclosed that the workplace culture prohibited or stalled their careers. Ethnically diverse employees also reported a wide range of racist experiences over the course of their careers, including microaggressions, systemic discrimination, structural barriers, and instances of institutional racialised practices.

As one of the first generation in my family to attend university and growing up in a relatively poor working-class household, I would not describe myself as coming from a privileged background.

As I stand at the apex of professional success, my career catapulting me into the ranks of the elite and my social circle filled with high achievers, my husband's entrepreneurial ventures further cementing our status, I am frequently categorised as middle-class. Yet, this designation feels like a fragile veneer, a societal construct that lacks true substance.

This is because, despite my numerous accomplishments, I am not perceived as an equal among my White peers. In the eyes of the world, my race is the primary and most defining trait, eclipsing all other aspects of my identity. It is a stark reality that any other attribute – my professional achievements, academic qualifications, my board-level appointments – is relegated to secondary status, considered only after the initial judgement based on the colour of my skin. This reality is punctuated by negative racialised experiences that serve as stark reminders that racial inclusion remains elusive.

Each interview revealed a sense of powerlessness, despair and indignity at racialised lived experiences of working and attempting to progress careers. The participants projected a sense of rejection which persisted despite high levels of educational attainment and relevant professional experience. My reflective memos revealed that, despite participants' numerous attempts to navigate different career pathways, they were consistently and frustratingly diverted into a cul de sac which blocked their career progression.

Whilst heading up several HR functions, I experienced racialised harassment and victimisation by line managers, colleagues and subordinate direct reports. What these incidents demonstrated was that, no matter how accomplished or senior a Black person may be, many people still see them as inferior due to ethnicity.

These incidents were emotionally draining, time-consuming and stressful, and resulted in the need to start over again in new organisations. These experiences resonated with the lived experiences of participants concerning the complexity of understanding the structural, institutional and systemic racism and Whiteness that impact on the career progression of Black professionals.

This was echoed by an incident reported by Black British *Vogue* editor Edward Enninful, in which a security guard at his own office did not recognise him and racially profiled him (BBC News, 2020).

Black professionals can reach their full potential when they are not stereotyped and discriminated against. However, I have found that the bumps in the road do not dissipate the more senior one becomes. Rather, there are new and more complex battles to overcome. Reflecting upon the research interviews, I was heartened that participants were so open and honest in sharing their innermost career experiences.

Respondents expressed gratitude for being able to share their career journeys and aspirations for the first time in their lives. I was saddened and appalled at the workplace experiences they had endured and felt some of the disclosures were tantamount to mental and psychological abuse. This caused me to further reflect upon the phenomenon of Black employees attending work and facing such daily hostility with little recourse for their plight to be addressed in any meaningful way.

What was being described is a form of racialised trauma which impacts on the mind, body and soul. As an HR professional, I am hopeful that this book will help to achieve some level of change in practice, as there is an urgency to address these issues head-on. The next section sets out the theories and models I developed as part of my doctoral research and moves us a step closer to the end goal – change.

From Research to Theory

The theoretical foundations of my research were based upon three pillars: the lived experiences of ethnically diverse employees; the link between race and career progression; and the intersection between HR management and diversity, equity and inclusion. Using constructivist grounded theory as the methodology, I developed six theoretical models which are discussed next.

Lived Experience

This research centred on the lived experience of ethnically diverse employees to understand the impact of workplace culture on career progression from their unique standpoints. The study revealed a mismatch between what companies aspire to achieve in DEI and the lived experience of ethnically diverse employees. From a critical race theory standpoint, a two-tier workforce has emerged where ethnically diverse employees encounter a hostile environment driven by anti-Black racism (Ross, 2020) creating barriers to progression. Meer (2018) posits that racial inequality is deliberate.

This study has shown that racial inequalities are not just deliberate but designed to create the worst of experiences for Black people and to do so in a pernicious way.

The research found that ethnically diverse employees had to navigate racism daily, did not have a voice in the workplace, generally had more qualifications than their White peers but were judged by different standards of competence and intelligence and were allocated heavier workloads with limited resources. The study further revealed the impact of ethnically diverse employees having zigzag careers as a result of structural racism.

The conceptual development of the lived experience of ethnically diverse employees led to theorising that, firstly, racial equity and inclusion approaches must be grounded in the lived experience of ethnically diverse employees, recognising the impact of anti-Black racism, White privilege and institutional Whiteness. This is depicted in Model 1. Failing to recognise this starting position is likely to lead to a reproduction of previous, ineffective solutions that have little impact on tackling systemic discrimination.

Model 1: Lived experience approach to racial equity and inclusion

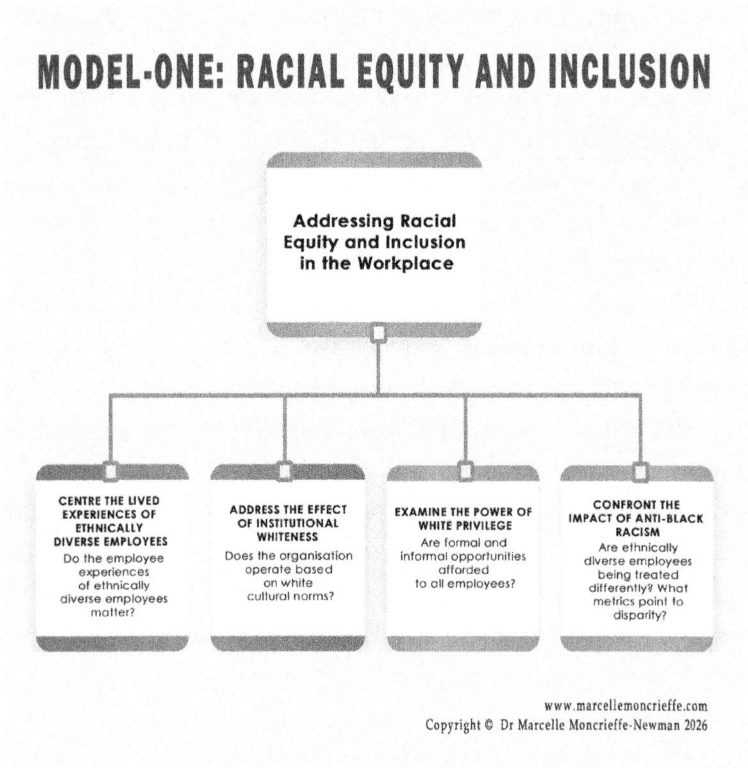

Secondly, organisations create a segregated and racialised career experience for ethnically diverse employees which results in a two-tier employee experience saturated with microsabotage. This is illustrated in Model 2.

Model 2: Two-tier employee experience for ethnically diverse employees

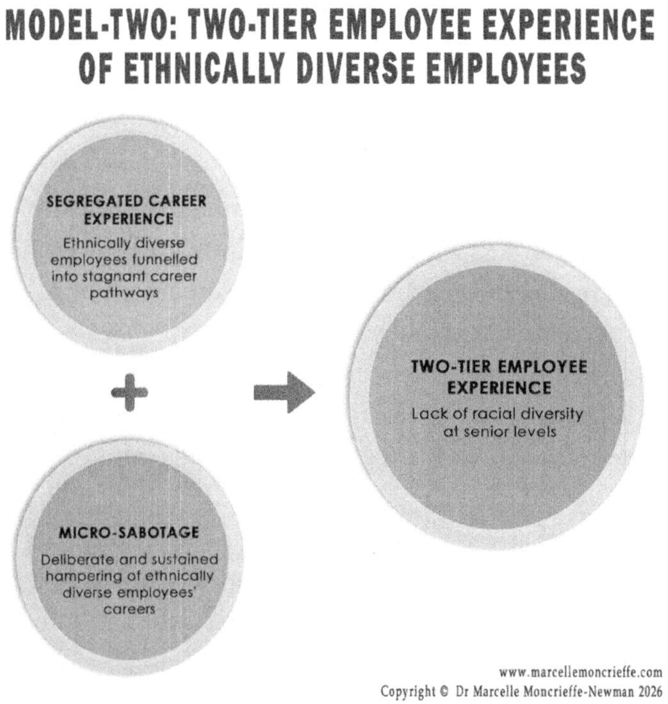

5.2.2 Organisational Culture

This research focused on the impact of organisational culture, as it relates to the career progression of ethnically diverse employees. The study found that ethnically diverse employees experience hostile, White-dominated environments. This resonated with research into Whiteness, racialised organisations and institutionalised racism enabled by spokespeople that deny it exists (Fekete, 2020). The research revealed that raising a racial discrimination complaint can be a slippery slope to the end of a Black employee's career.

Bullying and harassment occurred on the part of line managers, peers, direct reports and by proxy. In other words, bullying is transpiring from all fronts and there was little useful intervention from human resource managers and a notable lack of intervention from bystanders. Ethnically diverse employees were shut out of corporate succession planning and talent management. In so doing, corporate career progression functions were essentially reproducing what had gone before, with a lack of investment in Black talent. Consequently, ethnically diverse employees were funnelled into often dead-end, ethnically diverse development programmes.

Mentors and sponsors were accidental rather than purposeful and, in the case of sponsors, these were very rare; further, the poor treatment of Black leaders was off-putting for up-and-coming ethnically diverse employees. The study revealed it was not a case of 'not what you know, but who you know', as all that mattered was 'who White people know', and that unconscious bias training taught White people to hide their views and made no difference to career progression of ethnically diverse employees.

Theorising the impact of organisational culture on career progression led firstly to the concept of organisational exclusion from corporate talent management and succession planning due to a disregard and lack of interest in the careers of ethnically diverse employees. Secondly, hostile organisational environments, dominated by accepted institutional Whiteness and racism, blame ethnically diverse employees for their lack of career progress, utilising a deficit model. Thirdly, through custom and practice, organisations expect ethnically diverse employees to remain silent about their racially discriminatory treatment or risk punitive sanctions, whilst White privilege is hidden and unchallenged. This is represented in Model 3.

Model 3: Impact of organisational culture on ethnically diverse employees

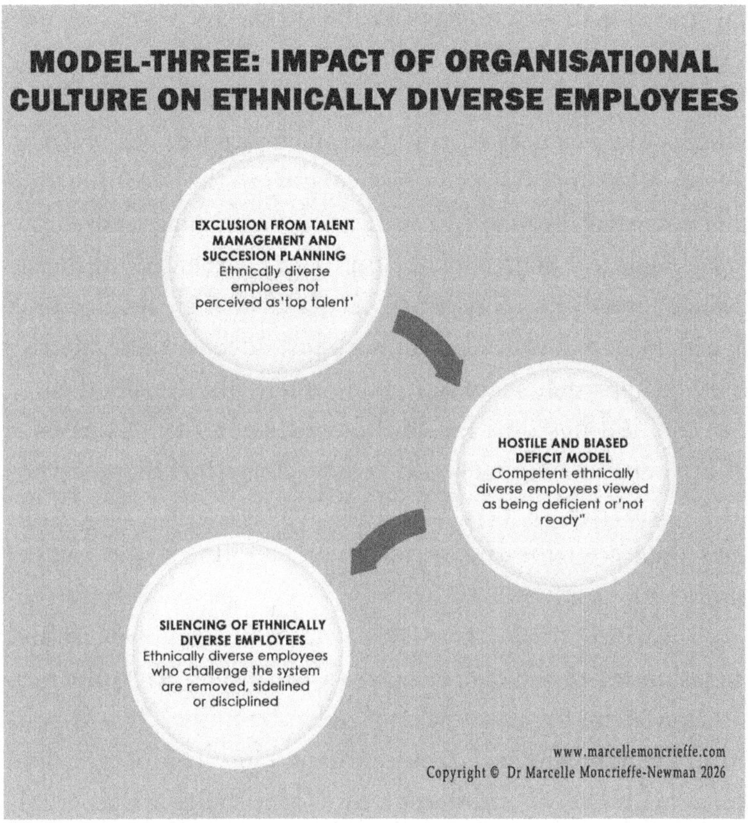

5.2.3 Human Resource Management and Diversity, Equity and Inclusion

The research sought to examine the role of HR managers in relation to the career progression of ethnically diverse employees. The study found that HR managers were ill-equipped to handle complaints of racial discrimination and bias and colluded with line managers to further victimise

Black complainants, and that HR intervention often made the situation worse, partly driven by HR maintaining the status quo and simply replicating the ineffective way race cases have always been handled.

HR was thus viewed as a key player in enabling poor career progression practices to continue unchallenged and was also found to be supporting and participating in the discrimination that occurred through informal recruitment practices, corporate talent and succession planning that excluded ethnically diverse employees, poor working practices that did not hold line managers and leaders to account, advocating ineffective training approaches and not taking action on diversity data.

The findings thus led to the conclusion of the existence of a woeful inadequacy and complacency in HR practitioners' expertise in diversity and inclusion, the shortcomings then contributing to the poor handling of race-based employment issues.

Theorising the intersection between HR and diversity and inclusion led to the concept that HR managers' lack of diversity and inclusion expertise and understanding of lived experience, in addressing racial discrimination in career progression, exacerbates the discrimination and contributes to poor HR policy and practice outcomes for ethnically diverse employees. Secondly, HR approaches to diversity and inclusion had not addressed underrepresentation of ethnically diverse employees in the workplace but, perversely, were contributing to it through reproduction of cultural norms. Lastly, HR managers reinforced and did not challenge the system of White privilege and did not understand the HR levers that enable or disable career progression of ethnically diverse employees. This theory is shown in Model 4.

Model 4: HR practitioner challenges

5.2.4 Impact of Racism

The research aimed to establish the link between race and career progression. The impact of racial discrimination was found to be devastating in terms of career outcomes, wellbeing, unequal pay, livelihoods, degrading treatment and self-confidence. Ethnically diverse employees described the experience as akin to psychological warfare with constant negative messages and an all-pervasive Whiteness that was never acknowledged or spoken about. The study revealed unequal pay was a major barrier to progression and that confronting it was met with denial and blame.

Conceptual development of the impact of race on career development led to the notion of careers being shaped by race. The study theorised that the racial barriers experienced were deliberate rather than accidental, proven by the findings demonstrating that the experience was replicated across different organisations.

This study found that racism was accepted in the workplace and that it came from all angles – line managers, direct reports, colleagues, policy application, practices and behaviour. Theorising the impact of race on career progression led to the concept that race is the dominant factor that shapes the careers of ethnically diverse employees and has resulted in a disappointing ethnicity career progression gap. This theory is illustrated in Model 5.

Model 5: Ethnicity career progression gap

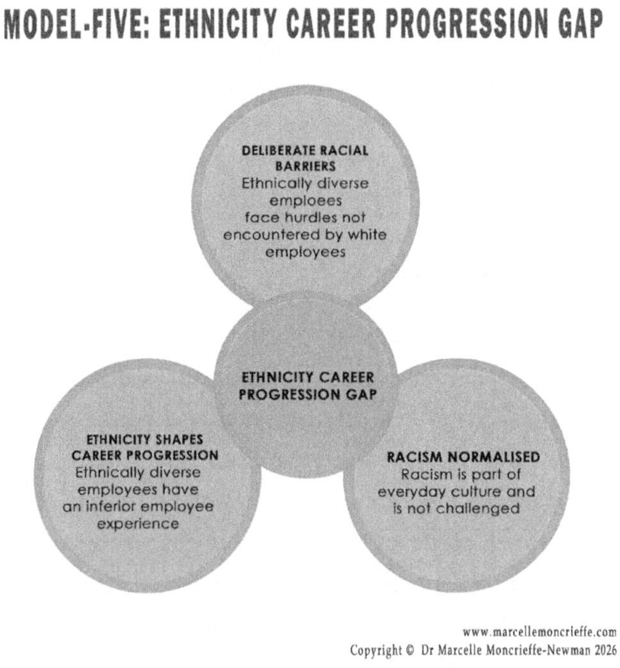

5.2.5 Creating a Culture of Racial Inclusion

So, what are the hallmarks of a racially inclusive workplace culture? The models I developed and presented throughout this section illustrated theoretical approaches which can help organisations to think about what factors may influence transformational change. I have developed these models further and translated them into a single model that organisations can use to create a culture of racial inclusion which is set out in the following steps and depicted in Model 6.

1. **Commitment to Anti-Racism:** Leadership actively engage in and promote anti-racist frameworks.
2. **Lived Experience Focus:** Develop initiatives that prioritise and amplify the experiences of Black and underrepresented employees.
3. **Equitable Employee Experiences:** Strive to eliminate disparities in employee experiences through positive action, ensuring equity across all ethnicities.
4. **Inclusive Talent Management:** Align talent-management and succession-planning strategies with established inclusion targets.
5. **Expertise in Equity and Inclusion:** Ensure that HR professionals possess the necessary knowledge and skills in equity and inclusion practices.
6. **Address Career Progression Gaps:** Implement systems to recognise, monitor and actively address the ethnicity career progression gap.

Model 6: Creating a culture of racial inclusion

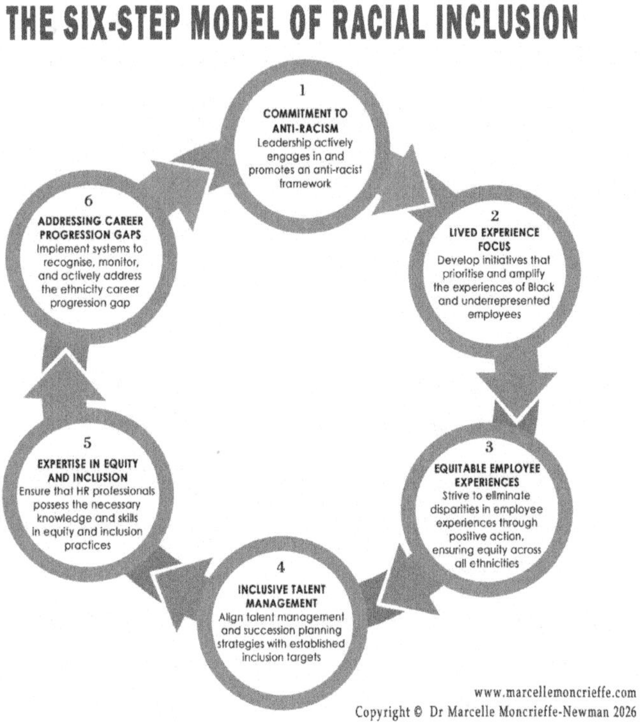

Changing HR Practices

My research found that HR practitioners were not equipped to handle racial discrimination complaints and, in some cases, they even participated in further mistreatment of ethnically diverse employees who raised concerns.

This highlights a structural problem and the need for HR practitioners to receive proper training and support to address racial discrimination in the workplace. My findings indicate that HR practice was seen as part of the problem, rather than the solution, and that Black employees were often subjected to indifference and ineffective internal complaint procedures. This lack of understanding and action on the part of HR practitioners only perpetuates the cycle of discrimination and reinforces the need for organisations to take active measures to address racism in the workplace.

Lack of expert HR guidance also impacted career progression of Black employees. HR practitioners were unable to influence discriminatory practices such as unfair hiring, biased career development plans and harmful work practices. There was a lack of understanding of effective development programmes for Black and ethnically diverse employees. HR practitioners were not doing enough to promote racial equity in the workplace.

HR practitioners may not realise that they are contributing to discrimination against non-White employees. This is due to what has been referred to as 'benevolent discrimination'. Romani et al. (2019) define 'benevolent discrimination' as 'a structural and subtle form of discrimination, whose perpetrators are blind to its effects', which in turn prohibits HR professionals 'from seeing how they contribute to ethnic discrimination'. 'HR Managers are blind to their role' in continuing discrimination against non-White employees because they are engaging in benevolent acts that position the othered group as inferior. This concept highlights the challenges people of colour face when trying to get help from HR for racial issues in the workplace.

Sensoy and DiAngelo (2017) suggest that hiring managers should acknowledge their role in the lack of equity progress in the workplace. They believe that everyone should realise that their role is not neutral. I believe this notion can also be applied to HR professionals. HR practitioners should understand their part in practices which enable unequal treatment in hiring, training and promotion for Black employees. By recognising this, HR professionals can improve both policy and practice and better support the career growth of global majority employees.

Only 3% of the participants in my study felt that their organisation's diversity and inclusion efforts were effective. Because of this, some of the participants I spoke to had lost hope of any meaningful change taking place.

Effective Allyship

An ally is 'a person who consciously commits, attitudinally and behaviourally, to an ongoing, purposeful engagement with and active challenging of White privilege, overt and subtle racism, and systemic racial inequalities for the purpose of becoming an agent of change in collaboration with, not for, people of color' (Erskine & Bilimoria, 2019).

After the Black Lives Matter protests, ethnically diverse staff reported unequal pay and promotion opportunities compared to their White counterparts. If leaders are unsure about how to respond, it's better to admit that the company doesn't have the answer, rather than make performative PR statements. Allies must be willing to actively fight against racism, not just express concern.

To address these issues, scholars have called for organisations to implement solutions such as activist allyship, anti-racist approaches and increased representation of ethnically diverse leadership. These solutions aim to dismantle systemic racism and create a more inclusive workplace culture. However, many organisations have yet to take these steps, leaving ethnically diverse employees feeling frustrated and unsupported.

Allyship can play a crucial role in creating positive change for Black and ethnically diverse employees. Allies must engage in ongoing self-reflection and critical analysis in order to resist oppressive ideologies and work towards social and self-transformation.

Allyship requires commitment and action, rather than just surface-level support. White people must be willing to actively advocate against racism, rather than just expressing moral sympathy. This includes speaking up when witnessing microaggressions or unequal pay, and actively working to dismantle systems of oppression. They must not, however, turn into White saviours.

It's important to note that allyship must be more than just optics. Companies must actively work to create a more inclusive workplace culture, rather than just making public statements to appear socially conscious. To facilitate this change, allies must be willing to educate themselves and engage in difficult conversations about race and discrimination.

Wellbeing of Black Employees

Perseverance will be a key requirement for Black employees seeking to progress their careers. Miriam Manderson in her book *From Hood to Headship* (2022) takes the reader through the journey of success in the face of adversity. In particular, Manderson describes the challenge of career rejection from the intersectional lens of a Black woman. Manderson shares the power of learning from experiences and of the greatness that can be achieved from not giving up.

Beyond the UK, Erskine et al. (2021:38) cite the low number of Afro-Diasporic women in the c-suite in America and articulate that their journeys are challenging and discouraging, and force them 'to approach their corporate careers with a mindset of surviving, enduring and coping, rather than thriving, while advancing to leadership'. Misogynoir, a term created by Bailey (Visibility Project, 2014), highlights the distinct methods used to pathologise Black women based upon anti-Blackness and misogyny. This causes them to navigate unwelcoming workplace environments, as well as 'being subjected to high emotional costs including spirit murder and emotional taxation' (Erskine et al., 2021:47). The concept of 'spirit murder' refers to the emotional cost of Black employees navigating unwelcoming workplaces which takes a toll on their spirit or mood.

To overcome this, Erskine et al. (2021:47) 'recommend strategies for Afro-Diasporic women to attain power currency as an ameliorative way to navigate the Black ceiling'. These findings stress the additional burden of Black employees navigating senior career progression and the impact these hurdles place on their health and wellbeing. Given the battle to achieve progress, it is even more remarkable when Black employees can overcome these obstacles and achieve career success.

In the early 2000s, Smith et al. (2007:555) coined the expression 'racial battle fatigue' which relates to 'the result of constant physiological, psychological, cultural, and emotional coping with racial microaggressions in less than ideal and racially hostile or unsupportive environments' (Embrick et al., 2017). In response, some organisations in the UK started to introduce wellbeing roles to support Black and ethnically diverse employees.

McCluney et al.'s 2017 study suggests that people of colour may be inclined to 'call in Black to work' when appalling examples of racial violence are witnessed or experienced and reflects upon the need to address the feelings of Black employees on an everyday basis in organisations 'that reinforce and reproduce systemic racism' (McCluney et al., 2020:50).

A pun on calling in sick, "calling in Black to work" refers to the trauma of these situations on Black people who may feel unable to attend, perform or be present at work in the wake of racial violence. It is asserted that racial violence is one cause of needing to call in Black to work but there are many others, including microaggressions, selective incivilities, structural racism and denial and indifference towards the overall lived experience of being Black at work. The scope of selective incivility was further broadened by Cortina et al. (2013) to recognise race and gender intersectionality, 'demonstrating that racialised women experience selective incivility more sharply and damagingly' (Ozturk & Berber, 2020:7).

The concept of 'weathering' describes the gradual decline of health for people from minoritised ethnic groups who experience enduring social and economic disadvantage due to racism and discrimination (Geronimus et al., 1992). This phenomenon has significant implications for the long-term health outcomes of Black and ethnically diverse people. Weathering is the cumulative impact of repeated exposure to racism and discrimination over time. This chronic stress leads to gradual deterioration of physical and mental health, premature ageing at the biological level and increased vulnerability to various health conditions.

Dr Arline T. Geronimus coined the term 'weathering', and found that the health of Black adults may begin to deteriorate prematurely compared to their White counterparts due to the cumulative impact of exposure to social and economic adversity (Geronimus et al., 1992; Stopforth et al., 2022). Dr David

R. Williams has noted that Black adults in the United States experience 'greater physiological wear and tear and are aging, biologically, more rapidly than [their White counterparts]' (Sandoiu, 2021).

From my research, and also reflecting on participants who have been through harrowing workplace discrimination ordeals, the importance of Black employees taking care of themselves cannot be stated strongly enough. I know many prominent professionals from the global majority who have suffered through long-lasting campaigns of racial discrimination that have impacted on all aspects of their wellbeing from mental to physical to financial. This has resulted in the need for counselling, coaching, healing, extended career breaks and utilisation of support networks.

In addition, many individuals have needed to change career, switch from permanent to interim roles or leave their job with nothing to go to. The most severe impacts have been on mental health and I have unfortunately witnessed people have mental health episodes as a result of the ill-treatment. The fight for justice is arduous and draining if one has the misfortune of trying to seek recompense through an employment tribunal or a settlement with their employer.

Lastly, given the challenges outlined above, Black employees need to be mindful of an organisation's ability to transparently support career progression and, therefore, need to promote their own capability. Self-management of career is important, including the use of independent external evaluation through informal mentors, as internal evaluation often undervalues Black employees' performance. Ethnically diverse employees should be encouraged to identify opportunities and development to facilitate that self-management which could include drawing on a range of internal and external opportunities, such as seeking a coach or mentor or joining specific networks.

I know there will be employees who feel stuck and many, if not all, who have responsibilities that mean they need to remain with their current employer. Despite the challenges, I want Black people to know that you are good at what you do, that what you are experiencing is temporary and that you will succeed and thrive in the right environment. Reach out to networks and realise that you are not alone. Seek out people who have your best interests at heart and maintain your self-confidence and belief in yourself. For employers, check-in with employees experiencing racial conflict and ensure that appropriate support is available. For additional resources, please see the useful links section at the end of the book.

Leadership

To address the underrepresentation of Black employees at senior levels in organisations, exceptional leadership at board and executive level is essential. This leadership must be characterised by a clear vision, a comprehensive understanding of best practices, and a commitment to transformational change.

Research indicates that many Black employees experience a lack of support, sponsorship and intervention from leaders, often facing discrimination from line managers and superiors. These conditions create workplace environments that are anti-Black, placing organisations at the lower end of the maturity spectrum in terms of being anti-racist institutions.

Dr Shereen Daniels (2022) puts forward a four-factor racial equity maturity model for organisations which provides a powerful tool to assess where organisations are now and where they aspire to be. At level four, which is the highest level, leaders are encouraged to influence positive change in anti-racist practices across their entire ecosystem. Dr Daniels (2022) proffers that essential leadership competencies to authentically respond to racism include moral courage, humility and tenacity.

Nazir Afzal's 2023 book *Race to the Top: How to fight structural racism* provides deep insights into the racialised experiences of Black and ethnically diverse people in the UK and focuses on the injustice baked into powerful industries and institutions. In his book, Afzal highlights the issue of fear that stops people in the public sector from speaking out, pointing out that senior individuals felt it would be career suicide to expose racism. I share his disappointment.

I agree with Afzal's contention that future leaders can be found in our local communities – they just need to be given the chance. However, what type of leadership qualities will achieve transformational change in creating inclusive work environments? I am a proponent of ethical and inclusive leadership.

The concept of ethical and inclusive leadership is crucial in this context. As Kellerman (2004) notes, bad leadership can be characterised as either ineffective or unethical. Ineffective leadership fails to produce change, while unethical leadership fails to distinguish between right and wrong. Either form of leadership is likely to impede the creation of an inclusive workplace culture and may result in a hostile environment for senior Black employees.

Drawing inspiration from Shonda Rhimes' book *The Year of Yes: How to Dance It Out, Stand in the Sun and Be Your Own Person* (2015), there is a need to normalise the presence of senior Black employees in UK organisations. Leaders must actively work to normalise the hiring and promotion of senior Black leaders within their organisations.

Daniel Kahneman's *Thinking Fast and Slow* (2011) emphasises the power of individual cases in teaching psychology, as incongruity is embedded and resolved in causal stories rather than statistics alone. This principle can be applied to understanding the experiences of Black employees. While statistical data, such as the McGregor-Smith report's finding of a £24 billion annual loss in productivity due to underutilisation of Black, Asian and minority ethnic talents, is important, it should be presented alongside the lived experiences of those affected by inaction.

The Chartered Institute for Personnel and Development (CIPD) serves as the leading professional body for Human Resources and people development. Over 20 years ago, I joined as a member when pursuing my Master's degree in Human Resource Management at Middlesex University.

I sat down with Peter Cheese, the Chief Executive of the CIPD, to discuss my research and gain his insights into the reasons behind the limited career progression for Black employees in UK workplaces. Reflecting on the past decade, Peter acknowledged that efforts toward achieving racial balance in senior roles have intensified but recognised there was still more needed. He noted a 'disconnect between espoused and actual experience', a finding echoed in my research. Despite advances in equity and inclusion over the past decade, significant challenges persist.

Peter described the complexities of racial inclusion, asserting that the lack of progress is 'addressable' yet remains a 'wicked problem'. He underscored the critical role of leadership in fostering inclusive cultures, stating that change is unlikely if leaders and managers 'don't understand it'.

On evidence-based approaches, he highlighted the importance of data in identifying systemic barriers and HR's role in understanding these, suggesting that HR practitioners had a 'lack of understanding' of the HR mechanisms that could impact underrepresentation of Black people rather than intentional bias. Peter emphasised the need to connect diversity and inclusion efforts with business outcomes, stating, 'we've got to be very clear as to what is actually happening. So, if Black people aren't advancing at the same rate, what's happening, what are the barriers? But we've also got to be very clear on why it is important that we address it.'

Addressing resistance to diversity initiatives, Peter noted that political and media-driven anti-woke rhetoric partly fuels pushback and stressed the importance of aligning diversity efforts with business goals. He observed that businesses acknowledge media pushback but remain committed to their inclusion programmes because 'we actually believe it's important'. He highlighted progress in a range of sectors where there is increasing recognition that inclusion and supporting diversity are vital for business success.

Peter also emphasised the role of data and evidence in driving change, stating, 'we haven't always been good enough at the evidence base' and recommended that HR professionals develop stronger analytical skills and data literacy.

Peter called for a more systemic and holistic approach to equity and inclusion, encouraging a comprehensive strategy. Critiquing the current methods, he pointed out that 'part of the challenge for the profession has been that we've not always been good at looking at things systemically and holistically. We tend to look at things in a bit too much of a silo.' Despite these challenges, Peter remains optimistic about the future of racial inclusion in UK workplaces and highlights the systemic approach that organisations need to take in order to tackle underrepresentation at senior levels.

Christina Brooks is Chief Executive of Ruebik, an inclusion-first talent attraction agency and diversity, equity and inclusion consultancy. I sat down with her and gained valuable insights into the current racial equity landscape as well as challenges faced in recent years. Her perspectives shed light on the complexities of equity and inclusion efforts in corporate environments.

The aftermath of George Floyd's murder in 2020 sparked a reactive approach to increasing Black representation in leadership positions. Christina notes, 'in the last five years following the murder of George Floyd in 2020, there has been an immediate reaction of helicoptering Black talent in across all parts of the business, but specifically at the leadership levels'. However, this approach has fallen short of addressing systemic barriers. Christina emphasises, 'we're going into the solve mode instead of looking at the environment in which these individuals are being placed'. Christina highlights the need for a deeper examination of organisational structures: 'what needs to be done is a real look at the systemic issues and barriers that exist within organisations'. This observation aligns with the experiences of many Black leaders who find themselves navigating hostile and unwelcoming environments. These challenges can manifest in various forms, including exclusion from decision-making processes, being sidelined and experiencing overt and subtle forms of discrimination.

Christina believes that a critical oversight in many organisations is the failure to connect diversity initiatives with broader business objectives. Christina points out that 'Organisations have forcibly said we need more Black leaders without tying it back to the commercial business case and value we bring, being reflective of customers and wider community and they are missing out on a trick.' Christina believes this disconnect can lead to superficial efforts that fail to create meaningful change. She reflected that, while representation is important, an excessive focus on numbers can be counterproductive and cautions: 'when you over-index on diversity metrics when filling vacancies, it can diminish the credibility of the candidates'. This approach risks reducing inclusion efforts to a mere tick-box exercise, without addressing the underlying cultural issues.

Christina advocates for greater involvement of external bodies in talent processes: 'there should be a lot more engagement with external bodies when it comes to the talent process until organisations really feel like they have what it takes to run an unbiased process'. Furthermore, she emphasises the importance of leadership accountability focused on behaviours and inclusion: 'Leadership accountability has to be taken into consideration where lack of representation is significant across leadership levels in an organisation. For me, this starts with exploration of leadership behaviours and attitudes towards inclusion in that culture.'

Christina believes that a fundamental step in addressing talent management is to engage with the affected groups. She stresses the need to 'listen to the affected community and listen to the affected group'. This approach ensures that equity and inclusion efforts are grounded in the lived experiences of underrepresented groups.

Christina highlights the transformative impact of sponsorship programmes: 'Sponsorship is key. It's a defining relationship that can unlock opportunity ... If you have an executive sponsor, or somebody who speaks on your behalf when you are not in the room, it can change the entire trajectory of your career.' This is an area highlighted in my research whereby Black employees were not benefitting from sponsorship, but in fact the opposite was true – they were often being sabotaged.

While acknowledging the slow pace of change, Christina sees potential for progress in the coming decades, 'Sadly, I don't think that we will see a huge shift in our lifetime … but the ground work is vital and we have laid a solid foundation. I hope our younger children, Generation Alpha, simply won't understand why there has been so much discrimination, but expect leadership positions to be measured by skills and competency only, without the historical barriers to entry.' She notes that the increasing volume of Black talent at mid-career levels may lead to changes in the next 10–15 years, albeit at a 'glacial pace'.

In conclusion, Christina believes that, while progress has been made in recognising the need for increased Black representation in senior roles, significant challenges remain. Organisations must address systemic issues, align diversity efforts with business strategy, and create truly inclusive environments to effect meaningful and lasting change. Clearly, the journey towards equitable representation and inclusive corporate cultures is ongoing, requiring sustained effort and commitment from all levels of leadership.

In an enlightening conversation with Jinjer Kandola MBE, Chief Executive of North London NHS Foundation Trust (NLFT), we delved into the complex issue of Black representation in senior NHS roles. As a board member of NLFT for several years, I've witnessed at first hand the Trust's forward-thinking approach to mental health services. However, Jinjer's insights reveal that, even in progressive organisations, the path to racial equity in leadership remains fraught with challenges.

Jinjer outlined the slippery slope of inclusion and expressed concern about a troubling trend in diversity efforts. 'I feel like we're slipping backwards and I kind of feel that as the economy is shrinking and as finances are tightening, [inclusion] almost becomes a little bit tokenistic.' This regression highlights the fragility of progress and the need for unwavering commitment to diversity initiatives, even in times of economic strain.

Jinjer reflected on the need to redefine talent and opportunity. A critical issue Jinjer identified is the narrow definition of 'talent' that often excludes ethnic diversity. 'We need to think about how we identify and nurture and support talent.' Jinjer felt there was a myopic view of Black and Asian professionals whereby they must prove their worth through experience, while their White counterparts are often given opportunities based on potential alone.

I have seen at first hand how this unfair standard on the application of 'potential' not only limits opportunities but also leads to a self-perpetuating cycle of underrepresentation and it is incredibly frustrating. This double standard manifests its way into recruitment processes, where Black and Asian candidates are frequently labelled as 'too operational', while White candidates are seen as having strategic potential. This resonates with the findings in my research and such biases create significant hurdles for ethnically diverse candidates aspiring to leadership roles.

Jinjer pointed out a stark contrast within the medical profession: the high number of Black nurses versus the low number of Black psychiatrists. This disparity underscores the systemic barriers that persist in career advancement for Black people in the NHS. The burden of exceptional performance is another trope that hinders career progression for Black and Asian employees; 'it is harder as a Black leader because the expectations are twice as high for you,' Jinjer stated, echoing a sentiment familiar to many professionals of colour.

Jinjer didn't shy away from addressing the elephant in the room: structural racism. 'We have organisations that have structural racism, [but] they don't always think [this is the case],' she observed. Problematically, organisational blindness to ingrained biases poses a significant obstacle to meaningful change. Jinjer advocates for moving beyond superficial 'tick box' exercises and investing in real, substantive solutions.

At NLFT, Jinjer has implemented positive internal talent-management strategies, creating clear career progression paths for ethnically diverse employees. However, Jinjer agreed there is a need to rethink HR and leadership accountability. Jinjer expressed reservations about current HR practices, particularly the business partner model. She raised a thought-provoking concern with the observation that business partners often become deeply integrated with the leadership team of the department they support. While this close alignment can foster understanding of departmental needs, it also carries a risk. Jinjer cautioned that this intimate involvement might lead HR partners to view people issues through a narrow, potentially biased lens.

'I do have a problem with the business partner model because when I [was] a business partner, I'm a partner of that management team,' Kandola explained. This perspective highlights the delicate balance HR professionals must strike between supporting leadership objectives and maintaining an impartial stance on employee matters. The risk lies in potentially compromising the broader, organisation-wide perspective that HR traditionally brings to people-management issues.

Jinjer's insight underscores the need for HR business partners to maintain a degree of independence and objectivity, even as they work closely with specific departments. It challenges organisations to rethink how they structure their HR functions to ensure fair and balanced people-management practices across the entire organisation. Jinjer emphasised that: 'individual leaders must have inclusion objectives they are individually accountable for in their area'. This approach shifts the responsibility for equity and inclusion from HR departments to all levels of leadership.

Reflecting on the aftermath of the Black Lives Matter movement, Jinjer cautioned against performative actions and tokenistic recruitment. While acknowledging progress in some organisations, she remains vigilant: 'I sometimes worry that diversity, equity and inclusion might go backwards as extreme views come to the fore.'

To chart a path forward, Jinjer proposed several actionable strategies which align with my recommendations. Firstly, sponsorship programmes: 'there is something about sponsorship of talented Black individuals by senior leaders,' she suggested, emphasising the importance of active mentorship and support. Secondly, rethinking recruitment: 'we've got to address the way we use head-hunters for various senior posts,' Kandola stated, advocating for more inclusive talent search processes. Thirdly, early career support: she stressed the importance of 'intentionally developing really nurturing strong relationships with schools and sponsoring people through university or a degree apprenticeship' to build an inclusive talent pipeline from the ground up. Lastly, expanded networking opportunities: Jinjer highlighted the need for broader and more mainstream networking and sponsorship opportunities for Black and Asian employees, particularly at senior levels.

In conclusion, Jinjer's insights reveal that achieving racial equity in NHS leadership requires a multifaceted, sustained effort. It demands not only structural changes but also a shift in organisational culture and individual mindsets. As the NHS continues to evolve, leaders like Jinjer are paving the way for a more inclusive and equitable future in healthcare leadership.

In the pursuit of a more equitable organisational landscape, leadership plays a pivotal role in addressing the glaring underrepresentation of Black employees in senior positions. Visionary leaders can spearhead profound change by integrating equity and inclusion strategies across all levels of their organisations. For individuals who are not Black, the journey to combat racism in the workplace begins with introspection.

It is crucial to reflect on past actions that may have contributed to a hostile environment for Black and ethnically diverse colleagues. Ask yourself: What motivated these actions? What impact did they have? And most importantly, what steps will you take to ensure a different, more inclusive path forward? This self-examination is the first step toward creating a workplace where everyone can thrive. Using the study notes section at the end of the book, you can utilise the following steps to instigate personal change.

1. **Acknowledge and Reflect:** Recognise past behaviours that may have harmed Black and ethnically diverse employees. Understand the motivations behind these actions and their impact.

2. **Educate Yourself:** Engage in continuous learning about racism and its manifestations in the workplace. This knowledge will empower you to identify and confront biases.
3. **Promote Inclusive Practices:** Advocate for policies and practices that actively support equity and inclusion. See more in Chapter 6.
4. **Lead by Example:** Demonstrate a commitment to inclusivity in your daily interactions. Encourage open dialogue and create an environment where everyone feels valued and heard.
5. **Hold Yourself and Others Accountable:** Establish clear consequences for discriminatory behaviour while creating a culture of accountability and respect.
6. **Listen to affected colleagues:** Make it a priority to actively engage with lived experiences and explore practical ways to demonstrate that people's voices are truly valued and heard.
7. **Gather accurate data:** Utilise up-to-date information to guide initiatives and support evidence-based decision making, ensuring actions are informed by reliable evidence.

By embracing these steps, you can become a catalyst for meaningful change, helping to dismantle the barriers that have historically excluded Black employees from leadership roles.

As has been highlighted, the lack of representation not only perpetuates systemic barriers but also limits the potential for ethnically diverse employees and the benefit of their contributions to inform decision-making at the highest levels. Leaders have the power to shape and set the tone for inclusive cultures. When senior executives demonstrate a genuine commitment to increasing Black representation in leadership, it sends a powerful message throughout the company.

Addressing the underrepresentation of Black employees at senior levels requires sustained commitment and action. By implementing comprehensive strategies and holding themselves accountable, leaders can create more inclusive environments where Black professionals have equitable opportunities to advance to senior positions. This not only benefits individual employees but also enhances organisational performance and innovation through diverse leadership perspectives.

Learning Points

The importance of carrying out this research utilising constructivist grounded theory was that it enabled a co-constructive approach which was important to illuminate the employee voice which is often missing. The methodology allowed me to gain deeper meaning through my own reflections and experiences as a Black woman. Using critical race theory (CRT) allowed the framing of the research through a vantage point of understanding the systemic and structural impact on the lived experience of ethnically diverse employees.

The research highlighted in this book revealed the prevalence of anti-Black racism and microsabotage in the careers of Black employees. Unfortunately, there is a chasm between the lived experience where 100% of participants experienced racism and, at the other end of the spectrum, the positive racial DEI values espoused by their employers.

Black employees perceived themselves to be spectators of pervasive White privilege and institutional Whiteness which operated as a standard phenomenon whereby White employees lacked understanding of their privileged path and did not understand the lives of people who were not privileged.

In other words, respondents observed that White employees were blind to their privilege whilst Black people were subject to a different set of rules and excluded from the chance to achieve their full potential. White privilege and institutional Whiteness were observed, felt and experienced by Black and ethnically diverse employees on a daily basis. The study found that low value was placed on qualifications of ethnically diverse employees, that they were judged according to higher standards of competence, allocated greater workloads, had important areas of work removed from them and were seen as dispensable.

The research revealed a lived experience of traumatic career journeys where poor behaviours meant that raising a complaint of racial discrimination often led to the end of ethnically diverse employees' careers. Black employees were often excluded from corporate talent-management and succession-planning schemes and instead funnelled into dead-end ethnically diverse development programmes or ignored completely.

Many of these programmes were based on a deficit model, often steeped in Whiteness, which did not acknowledge structural and systemic racism as being the cause of lack of career progression and, in some cases, were found to have a damaging impact on the Black attendees. Sponsorship was not routinely offered to ethnically diverse employees and unconscious bias training was found to be a diversion from the conscious and blatant racism that was in existence.

Racism isn't hiding in the shadows of unconscious thought – it's standing boldly in the light, unapologetically overt and deeply entrenched in tradition. Yet, society has developed a dangerous habit of cloaking it with euphemistic labels like 'unconscious bias', softening its impact and allowing it to thrive unchecked. It's time to strip away these comforting illusions and confront racism for what it truly is: racism, i.e. the unfair treatment or judgement of people based on skin colour, ethnicity, or cultural background.

The term 'unconscious bias' has become a convenient shield, enabling excuses like: 'I didn't mean it that way', 'I wasn't aware I said that', or 'I acted without realising …' These deflections don't absolve responsibility – they perpetuate the problem. They create a mirage, a false narrative that normalises racism in workplaces and beyond, letting it blend seamlessly into the fabric of everyday life.

However, this mirage must shatter. The veil must be lifted to expose the truth: racism isn't unconscious; it's deliberate, systemic and deeply ingrained. By continuing to use language that softens its reality, we allow the status quo to persist. It's time to call it out, to name it boldly, and to dismantle the structures that enable its survival. Only then can we begin to build a future where equality isn't an aspiration but a lived reality.

My research found that HR practitioners often lacked the expertise or appetite to handle racial discrimination complaints, colluded with line managers to secure biased outcomes and were viewed as part of the system of institutional racism. Moreover, the study revealed that HR practitioners were often part of the system of White privilege and institutional Whiteness.

Therefore, some HR practitioners reinforced the system of privilege instead of challenging it. Participants observed that HR professionals felt the systems were transparent and fair. However, there is a need for the HR profession to recognise its role in practices that are complicit in career regression for Black employees and to prioritise gaining expertise in equity and inclusion solutions.

Equity and inclusion departments are not fit for purpose unless their intended outcomes impact on cultural change and transformation. There was a lack of external scrutiny of organisational equity and inclusion in relation to ethnicity and organisational equity and inclusion practice was found to be outdated.

The results of my research show that racism and bias pervade all aspects of career progression for Black employees, with racism leading them to breaking point. However, despite the positive equity and inclusion statements, widespread racism is generally accepted in workplaces, including many cases of unequal pay.

Further, the study found that career progression in the workplace is difficult once racism has been challenged. Whiteness in UK workplaces was found to be pervasive and tangible, yet invisible at the same time, and its existence needs to be accepted by organisations in order for it to be addressed. Lastly, the impact on wellbeing of ethnically diverse employees cannot be underestimated and a review of the wellbeing of this group of staff is necessary.

Summary

In conclusion, the lived experience of Black employees in the UK is dominated by negativity and discrimination. While activism, anti-racist approaches and increased representation of Black leadership can help create positive change, Allyship must also play a crucial role. Allies must engage in ongoing self-reflection, education and action in order to dismantle oppressive systems and create a more inclusive workplace culture.

Allies should be seen and not heard. My husband once told me that he had worked at an organisation where, in an open plan office, some staff had an 'Ally' flag to let staff know they were allies and available to help. This is not recommended!

The co-constructed solutions illuminated the participants' desire for organisations to engage in an active anti-racist approach that centred on the lived experiences of Black employees, starting with acknowledgement of the existence of racial bias. Scrutiny of the treatment of Black employees was needed as participants had experienced hostile cultures manifested in disregard, born out of anti-Blackness. Participants expressed the view that the CEO was responsible for diversity and inclusion and that all leaders should be active anti-racism advocates.

Organisations should review the way structural racism and microaggressions impact upon the career progression and employee experience of Black employees. Participants conveyed that, where Black employees are in senior positions, organisations should have a duty of care to ensure they are not bullied, harassed or discriminated against.

In the pursuit of genuine progress, it's crucial for organisations to discern between two distinct types of Black leaders. On the one hand, there are those who genuinely champion the advancement of other Black professionals, nurturing an environment of support and inclusivity. These are the vast majority of Black leaders. On the other hand, there exists a small minority of Black leaders who prioritise self-promotion over collective empowerment, often at the expense of their peers.

It's essential to make this distinction, as a small number of Black individuals may inadvertently perpetuate racist structures by acting as gatekeepers of systemic racism against other Black people. These individuals often serve as unwitting overseers of Whiteness, complicit in the racism that surrounds them.

So, how can one identify these self-serving leaders? They are often characterised by their actions: they undermine other Black leaders, presenting themselves as champions of inclusion while failing to take meaningful steps to develop current or future Black talent. In their organisations, Black voices are frequently silenced, and their primary focus is on personal advancement, even if it means sacrificing the wellbeing of others.

For the vast majority of ethical and inclusive Black leaders, participants expressed the view that their career progression should be tracked and succession-planning approaches reviewed to eliminate bias.

It was also found that sponsorship and mentoring should be purposeful. Underrepresentation from board level down was a priority area. Participants conveyed that positive discrimination should be considered along with targets for numbers of Black senior staff and accreditation.

HR practitioners were viewed as exacerbating discriminatory practices and needed to have DEI expertise to enable an effective review of HR interventions. Participants observed that DEI teams should adopt an organisational development approach.

The insidious nature of racism gives me pause and much food for thought. If we smell something fishy on the bias front in our workplace, what should be done? Whilst we are led to believe that the world is our oyster, how do Black people know if the next company will be worse than the current one when making a career move? In terms of what organisations can do next, the next chapter sets out recommendations.

CHAPTER 6

BEYOND LIP SERVICE – TURNING TALK TO ACTION

Change will not come if we wait for some other person or some other time. We are the ones we've been waiting for. We are the change that we seek.

Barack Obama

Creating a Culture of Racial Inclusion

This journey has yielded profound insights into the complexities of culture and racism. Arriving at this point is a testament to considerable perseverance and genuine engagement with challenging truths, many of which are often avoided. Your dedication to exploring these realities is commendable. Thank you for your commitment to this important journey.

Unfortunately, it is very real, and here we are. Now, on to the easy part, the dreaded 'so what?' moment. What can we actually do with all this information? How do we move from nodding sympathetically to, you know, doing something?

Well, here's the good news: my research has produced tangible, actionable insights which is more than can be said for many corporate diversity statements. It provides a roadmap for organisations that are genuinely interested in closing the ethnicity career progression gap, not just slapping a stock photo of ethnically diverse employees on their website. It also offers guidance for those ready to challenge the deeply embedded cultural and systemic norms that keep boardrooms looking like exclusive golf clubs.

The reality? Racial discrimination isn't just present in UK organisations, it's woven into the fabric, so much so that it's become an unspoken workplace norm. It's there in hiring decisions, promotions, 'cultural fit' excuses, and the well-timed interruptions in meetings. And yet, when Black employees voice their experiences, the reaction is often one of shock and confusion, as if racism is some distant historical relic rather than a daily reality.

But let's not despair (too much). There is a way forward. And because accountability is all the rage these days, it's time to talk about real workplace change.

Using the 'Creating a Culture of Racial Inclusion' model I introduced in Chapter 5, I will now take you through six –yes, six! – concrete steps to ensure that diversity isn't just a catchy HR slogan, but an actual, lived reality in your organisation. Let's get to work. Or, at the very least, let's try to do more than just talk about it.

Step 1. Commitment to Anti-Racism

Ethical and inclusive leadership is required at board and executive level to achieve sustainable change.

A. Leadership actively engages in and promotes an anti-racist framework

   - *Develop a Race Equality Action Plan*

- *Carry out a Racial Disparity Audit – to include a comprehensive data analysis of demographic representation at all levels; hiring and recruitment metrics (who gets hired, who doesn't); pay and promotion gaps, retention and attrition, performance evaluations*
- *Acknowledge the existence of racial bias within the organisation*
- *Centre the lived experiences of ethnically diverse employees*
- *Scrutinise the treatment of ethnically diverse employees to address hostile cultures*

To fix the ethnicity career progression gap, organisations must finally acknowledge that institutional, systemic, structural and modern-day racism aren't just figments of overactive imaginations. Instead of treating diversity like a PR stunt, they'll need to adopt a genuine anti-racist approach.

Firstly, accept that the problem isn't 'pipeline issues' or 'a lack of qualified candidates' but deeply ingrained workplace bias that keeps leadership teams racially undiverse. Secondly, actually do something about it. By introducing a comprehensive Race Equality Action Plan – a structured, measurable, and (hopefully) not-forgotten part of the company's Equity and Inclusion Strategy.

Because here's the thing: change won't happen through well-meaning diversity panels alone. It requires dismantling the policies and power structures that keep racial equity stuck in the 'nice to have' category rather than the 'we are actually serious about this' category. And yes, that means accountability, transparency and fewer excuses disguised as 'learning journeys'.

The real challenge rests with organisational maturity. To truly tackle racial disparities, instead of just rebranding the same old diversity efforts with fancier buzzwords, organisations must embrace ethical and inclusive leadership which, believe it or not, means actually listening to and centring the lived experiences of ethnically diverse employees. Revolutionary concept, I know!

Where to start? Acknowledge that racial bias exists. Yes, even here. Even in your organisation. Even if you've had a 'Black History Month Lunch & Learn' last year. The problem isn't just a few bad apples; it's the all-pervading Whiteness that's so deeply woven into workplace culture it's practically invisible – except, of course, to those being directly harmed by it.

B. Implement anti-racist leadership
   - *Set and monitor ethnicity representation targets*
   - *Apply anti-racist principles throughout the leadership chain*
   - *Target underrepresented groups for board and executive positions*

Leaders must hold themselves to account for setting ethnicity representation targets and monitoring ethnicity career progression. Adopting a suitable anti-racist approach should apply throughout the chain of distributed leadership, including senior leaders, line managers, recruiting managers, HR and DEI specialists. Underrepresented groups should be targeted for board and executive positions, reflecting the workforce, customer and general population demographics.

If organisations are serious about DEI, it's time to put their boards to work. As outsiders, they have the objectivity (and power) to enforce real change, and not just applaud diversity reports.

Boards should hold leadership accountable, scrutinise hiring, pay and promotions, and ensure DEI isn't just a tick-box exercise. Without real consequences, diversity remains a polite discussion topic, not a priority.

C. Establish sponsorship programmes

- *Facilitate formal sponsorship of ethnically diverse employees by leaders*
- *Define clear outcomes for sponsorship programmes*
- *Implement reciprocal mentoring initiatives*

Organisations should facilitate their leaders to become formal sponsors for ethnically diverse employees and sponsorship should be purposeful with well-defined outcomes such as addressing underrepresentation. Ethnically diverse employees should have role models they can respect and relate to, who support them in their career journey, and reciprocal mentoring should also be considered.

D. Strengthen definitions of racial discrimination

- *Recognise modern-day forms of racial discrimination*
- *Review approach to racial discrimination cases*
- *Utilise external inclusion experts where appropriate*

Organisations should define racial microaggressions and selective incivilities as a form of harassment in their anti-bullying policies. Harassment and bullying and grievance complaints centred on race should be examined to ensure that they are not being investigated through the lens of Whiteness, and external ethnically diverse DEI experts should be used to carry out race-centred investigations where none are available internally.

E. Allocate resources for ethnicity career progression
   - *Ring-fence specific resources to address historical career progression gaps*
   - *Utilise employee resource groups effectively*

Leaders should consider resources being specifically ring-fenced to address the historic ethnicity career progression gaps experienced by ethnically diverse employees and utilise appropriately equipped employee resources groups.

Step 2. Lived Experience Focus

Develop initiatives that prioritise and amplify the experience of Black and underrepresented groups.

A. Lived experience actions
   - *Align organisational values with the actual experiences of ethnically diverse employees*
   - *Regularly assess and improve the employee experience for all groups*

The lived experience of ethnically diverse employees should reflect the espoused diversity and inclusion values of the organisation; otherwise, the diversity and inclusion values are purely performative, meaningless and further contributing to anti-Black racism.

B. Create safe working environments
   - *Recognise and address toxic cultures where racial harassment thrives*
   - *Implement strict policies to confront and remove racist bullies*
   - *Focus on inclusive culture and organisational development*

Leaders must recognise and address pervasive and toxic cultures where racial harassment can thrive, and confront, punish or remove racist bullies and those complicit in continuing such destructive environments. A culture of inclusion supported by organisational development programmes means inclusion is embedded into working practices.

Step 3. Equitable Employee Experience

Strive to eliminate disparities in employee experiences through positive action, ensuring equity across all ethnicities.

A. Equity in application of career-related policies and practice
   - *Implement transparent career pathways and monitor metrics*
   - *Ensure equity of performance evaluation process*
   - *Review employee relations policy and practice*

Organisations must move away from 'segregated two-tier employee experiences' for ethnically diverse employees whereby career progression is slow and trust is low. What should no longer be tolerated is a normative Black lived experience of the workplace where racial bullying and harassment from line managers, peers, direct reports and by proxy are executed in the form of unfair performance management, exclusion from opportunities, threats and being exited from organisations.

B. Implement organisational development programmes

- *Design programmes that achieve cultural and behavioural change in anti-racism*
- *Learn from the lived experiences of ethnically diverse employees to inform these programmes*

To move towards an inclusive employee experience for all employees, rather than a two-tier racialised approach, organisations should implement organisational development which achieves cultural and behavioural change in anti-racism, anti-microsabotage, belonging and inclusivity by learning from the lived experience of ethnically diverse employees. Ethnically diverse employees should not be subjected to a separate inferior track, required to adhere to a different set of rules and excluded from achieving their full potential.

C. Provide comprehensive anti-racism training

- *Prioritise expert-led, face-to-face anti-racism training*
- *Cover topics such as institutional Whiteness, microaggressions and systemic racism*
- *Replace ineffective unconscious bias training with more impactful approaches*

Organisations should prioritise expert face-to-face anti-racism training to provide confidence and professionalism in dealing with complaints/problematic lived workplace experiences of underrepresented groups; this should be sponsored by senior leadership teams. This training should form part of a broader approach to organisational development which covers institutional Whiteness (including White privilege), microaggressions, anti-Black racism, systemic/structural racism, the role of bystanders, activist allyship and dispelling the myth of meritocracy.

This approach should replace unconscious bias training which can have the effect of teaching White employees to hide their views and does not aid Black employees' career progression.

D. Supportive environment for senior Black leaders
   - *Recognise Black leaders as role models*
   - *Examine differential treatment*

Where an organisation does have senior Black leaders, they should be viewed as role models for aspiring Black employees and as such there should be a special duty of care not to racially harass, bully or discriminate against them because of the colour of their skin, so as not to discourage other Black employees from seeking promotion or advancement.

Step 4. Inclusive Talent Management

Align talent-management and succession-planning strategies with established inclusion targets.

A. Review talent management against inclusion objectives
   - *Review and revise talent-management and succession-planning processes*
   - *Set targets for progression at every level*

- *Track key performance indicators to build a robust diverse talent pipeline*

Recognising that there are both formal and informal routes to career progression, organisations need to review their approach to talent management, succession planning and promotion, which includes tracking the outcomes of both routes on ethnically diverse employees to eliminate bias. This includes monitoring career progression of ethnically diverse employees, including the makeup of the talent pool, targets for progression at every level and tracking key performance indicators to build a robust Black talent pipeline.

B. Create transparent career pathways
- *Acknowledge the impact of discrimination on career histories*
- *Educate recruitment agencies and hiring managers on non-linear career patterns*

Organisations should create transparent career pathways that acknowledge the impact of discrimination on ethnically diverse employees' career history, performance and working time lost in fighting discrimination. Recruitment agencies, head-hunters and recruiting line managers should be aware of the underlying causes of non-traditional career patterns of Black candidates rather than judging them against the more linear career paths of White candidates. Organisations should reconsider the value placed on postgraduate education of ethnically diverse employees, particularly where there has been a lack of career progression.

C. Revise performance management and reward systems

- *Review appraisal and reward processes for bias*
- *Create clear equity and inclusion expectations in competency frameworks*

Organisations should review appraisal, performance management, recognition and reward processes to understand whether outcomes are biased and hold all line managers to account for diversity in their teams through creation of equality, diversity and inclusion objectives, starting with the chief executive. Behavioural, competency and performance frameworks should be clear on the equity and inclusion expectations of all employees.

D. Reform pay frameworks

- *Develop robust action plans to address ethnicity pay gaps*
- *Review hiring practices that continue pay discrimination*

Organisations should not only publish ethnicity pay gap data but reform mechanisms that enable pay discrimination. This includes pay on promotion, pay for additional responsibilities, annual reviews, performance bonuses and recognition payments, in addition to new starter salaries.

E. Implement effective Positive Action initiatives

- *Design Positive Action programmes with measurable objectives and outcomes*
- *Ensure senior leader accountability*
- *Regularly review the impact of such initiatives*

Positive Action programmes should have tangible benefits for participants and commit to tracking progress long-term. Development programmes should have measurable objectives and outcomes; not be reliant upon a deficit model; acknowledge structural racism; appoint ethnically diverse experts as well as employees with lived experience in their design; ensure senior leaders engage with participants, conduct regular progress reviews and take ownership of the outcomes.

Leaders should enable proactive agency in ethnically diverse employees, which encourages them to be their authentic selves at work and provides the right to challenge systemic race issues without fear of being reprimanded or dismissed. Ethnically diverse employees should remain part of mainstream talent management in addition to participating in Positive Action initiatives.

Step 5. Expertise in Equity and Inclusion

Ensure that HR professionals possess the necessary knowledge and skills in equity and inclusion practices. HR professionals and line managers have significant roles in determining acceptable conduct and practice, which needs to be reinforced through standards and frameworks.

A. Enhance HR expertise in equity and inclusion
   - *Develop specialised training for HR professionals in handling racial discrimination complaints*
   - *Review and improve ethnic representation within the HR function*

The lack of HR expertise to handle complaints of racial discrimination and the role of HR in the lack of career progression of ethnically diverse employees must be addressed. The HR function's role in reinforcing the system of privilege must be recognised in order to disrupt this practice. HR generalists need to be experts in equity and inclusion to ensure accountability at the right levels of the organisation. The racial makeup and representation of the HR profession should be prioritised for review as ethnic underrepresentation in the profession can compound the problem.

B. Develop HR practice

  - *Examine cultural norms and challenge the system*

Review HR practice through examining outcomes of employee relations cases, recruitment data and metrics which focus on career progression. Develop professional practice which provides expert advice on inclusive people-management practices.

Step 6. Addressing Career Progression Gaps

Implement systems to recognise, monitor and actively address the career progression gap.

A. Monitor the ethnicity career progression gap

  - *Regularly monitor career progression by ethnicity*
  - *Hold leaders accountable for diversity at all levels in their teams through specific objectives*

Organisations should review how microaggressions and other forms of racism impact on career progression. The 'ethnicity career progression gap' needs to be addressed and monitored, with the right expertise and support, throughout the chain of distributed leadership, including senior leaders, line managers, recruiting managers, HR and DEI specialists.

B. Utilise diversity-monitoring data effectively
   - *Measure and track progress of underrepresented groups*
   - *Use data to disrupt biased processes and achieve systemic cultural change*

Equity and inclusion practices must measure and track progress of underrepresented groups and take positive action to disrupt biased processes that reproduce historical outcomes. Equity and inclusion strategies should be transformational and achieve systemic cultural change.

By implementing these strategies, organisations can work towards creating more inclusive environments and addressing the ethnicity career progression gap. It's crucial to approach these initiatives with commitment, transparency and a willingness to make meaningful sustainable organisational changes.

Raising Your Game

If your organisation is further along the journey of racial inclusion and you want to know what to do next, the following actions can elevate your organisation to achieve best-in-class status:

Board-level actions

Mandatory board-level racial equity training

Require boards to undergo intensive, expert-led anti-racism training, ensuring those in power understand systemic barriers before setting inclusion strategies.

Board diversification
Review the composition of the board to ensure it reflects the diversity and perspectives of both the organisation's customers and employees.

Supply chain actions

Racial equity in procurement and supplier diversity
Implement policies that prioritise Black-owned and ethnically diverse businesses in procurement.

Leadership actions

Real consequences for failing DEI metrics
Tie executive bonuses and performance reviews to racial equity progress, making inclusion a business-critical issue, not an optional commitment.

Targeted leadership development for Black employees
Create executive fast-track programmes to combat underrepresentation in senior leadership, ensuring Black talent is actively sponsored.

Revise whistle-blowing procedures for racial discrimination
Establish independent reporting mechanisms.

Human Resources actions

Transparency in pay and promotion decisions
Require real-time ethnicity pay audits and publish promotion rates by ethnicity to prevent discriminatory progression barriers.

Anti-racism certification for HR professionals
Ensure HR teams receive anti-racism training so they stop reinforcing biased practices.

Systemic review of workplace language and norms
Identify and eliminate coded language that reinforces racial exclusion (e.g. 'cultural fit') and introduce inclusive performance assessment criteria.

Wellbeing actions

Address racial trauma in the workplace
Offer therapeutic support and wellbeing initiatives specifically for Black employees facing racialised workplace stress.

How to Implement a Culture of Racial Inclusion

There are effective strategies for embedding racial inclusion within everyday working practices, and it is likely that your organisation already has some foundations in place. In this section, I will share practical approaches and proven methods to further advance inclusion in your workplace.

1. **Align with Core Business Objectives**
   - Integrate the Race Equality Action Plan (REAP), along with equity and inclusion, as core priorities within the overall business strategy
   - Embed racial disparity audits in the same way as financial audits
   - Set specific, measurable targets for ethnicity representation, treating them like any other business KPI

2. **Demonstrate Visible Commitment**
   - Regularly communicate the organisation's anti-racist values and progress to all employees

- Publicly commit to action and share steps taken to demonstrate transparency and accountability

3. **Implement Structural Changes**
    - Revise HR processes to ensure unbiased application
    - Conduct comprehensive audits of hiring practices, pay equity and promotion criteria
    - Implement diverse hiring panels and fair recruitment processes
    - Create transparent and inclusive career pathways and talent-management processes

4. **Establish Formal Programmes**
    - Design and implement formal sponsorship programmes for underrepresented employees
    - Provide structured curriculums and resources to support sponsor–sponsee relationships
    - Create reciprocal mentoring initiatives to foster understanding across different groups

5. **Cultivate Inclusive Leadership**
    - Develop anti-racist leadership training as part of leadership framework, covering topics like institutional Whiteness and systemic racism
    - Encourage leaders to create safe spaces for open discussions about race and inclusion, alongside other employee fora
    - Model anti-racist behaviour by taking a proactive and visible stance

- Call out racist assumptions and intervene if witnessing a racist incident
- Hold colleagues accountable for their words and actions

6. **Link to Performance and Compensation**
   - Link executive compensation to improving representation of underrepresented groups
   - Include anti-racism and diversity objectives in senior managers' performance frameworks

7. **Allocate Resources**
   - Ring-fence specific resources to address historical career progression gaps for underrepresented groups
   - Invest in long-term, sustainable support, including pro-bono volunteerism and board service

8. **Leverage Existing Assets**
   - Use employee resource groups effectively to support inclusion initiatives
   - Utilise the organisation's intranet, newsletter or community pages to share anti-racism resources and education

9. **Monitor and Evaluate**
   - Track progress, gather feedback and implement actions from lived experiences of underrepresented groups
   - Implement regular reporting to monitor employee experience and attrition for underrepresented groups

10. **Adjust Strategies**
    - Be willing to adapt strategies based on feedback and measured outcomes

By integrating these recommendations, organisations can create a more racially inclusive environment that not only addresses systemic inequalities but also drives innovation and success.

Racial Inclusion Initiatives

We have explored the ways to create a culture of racial inclusion, and we have examined practical methods for implementing these changes in your organisation. You may be doing some of these things already, which is great. At this point, you may be wondering whether these actions will achieve greater equity for underrepresented groups in your organisation.

Well, in recent years, numerous organisations have successfully implemented racial inclusion initiatives. This section highlights notable examples from both the private and public sectors, demonstrating the range of approaches taken to address racial inclusion.

Private Sector Initiatives

Global Investment Company

A global investment firm with 8,000 employees implemented several strategies to promote equity and inclusion:

- Facilitated open dialogues on equity and inclusion led by thought leaders and experts
- Created safe spaces for employees to share experiences with leadership and colleagues

- Enhanced Employee Resource Groups to foster a greater sense of belonging
- Provided anti-racism educational resources
- Utilised internal social media to offer:
    - Mental health and wellness information
    - Personal accounts of colleagues' experiences with racism
    - Educational resources on systemic racism

Large Accounting Firm

One of the major accounting firms developed a comprehensive action plan to combat racial injustice and support Black professionals:

- Implemented six specific actions to address racial injustice
- Improved company-wide diversity and inclusion efforts
- Embedded community engagement through donations of time to social justice organisations
- Provided employees with one week of paid time annually for nonprofit volunteering
- Supported skills development for students and teachers in underserved communities
- Offered free racial trauma counselling for employees and their families
- Encouraged employee participation in inclusion networks and bias training

Financial Services Company
A financial services company took several steps to affirm its commitment to racial inclusion:

- Held listening sessions with clients and employee resource groups
- Provided communication kits for managers to encourage team dialogue
- Established Juneteenth as a paid holiday for US employees

Committed to measuring progress in hiring, promotion and retention of ethnically diverse colleagues

Public Sector Initiatives

Large Government Department
A major government department implemented a comprehensive Race Equality Action Plan (REAP) that achieved significant results:

- Increased Black and ethnically diverse representation from 14% to 16% in 16 months
- Boosted senior diverse representation from 9.6% to 11.2%
- Engaged nearly 50,000 colleagues in race equality learning
- Conducted a race disparity audit to identify areas for improvement

National Health Service (NHS)

The NHS has taken several steps to promote racial inclusion:

- Launched the Patient and Carer Race Equality Framework (PCREF) Partnership initiative
- Collaborated with Black-led voluntary and community sector organisations
- Implemented fair shares funding for community organisations
- Provided seats for community representatives on influential boards
- Co-created a redesigned peer support worker pathway
- Tracked race data through the workforce race equality standard

In addition, as discussed earlier, the North London NHS Foundation Trust has focused on career pathways and talent management of Black, Asian and underrepresented groups.

UK Civil Service

The UK Civil Service has made progress through various initiatives:

- Established diversity internship programmes for students from ethnically diverse backgrounds
- Implemented the Future Leaders scheme to accelerate development of ethnically diverse participants
- Created mentoring schemes targeting civil servants from different backgrounds
- Appointed permanent secretaries as 'diversity and inclusion champions'

- Increased the proportion of ethnically diverse staff in senior positions year-on-year over a four-year period

Key Drivers for Change

Based on experience, the primary catalysts for change in organisations include:

1. Addressing reputational risks linked to racial discrimination or a non-inclusive workplace culture
2. Desire to capture and improve metrics that show there is disparity between different groups of the workforce
3. Listening to lived experiences of underrepresented groups
4. Targeting specific areas holding the organisation back, such as:
    - Engrained racialised practices
    - Inappropriate hiring/promotion processes
    - Poor leadership behaviours
5. Responding to the expectations of Gen Z, tomorrow's leaders, who demand a contemporary, inclusive working environment

It is crucial to assess the cultural environment, as change begins at the micro-level with individuals. Connecting individuals to the necessary behavioural changes is essential for creating inclusive cultures where all employees can thrive. For more ideas on how to embed racial inclusion, refer back to the six models outlined in Chapter 4.

Organisations may adopt approaches similar to those outlined above or develop a combination of strategies depending on their progress towards becoming racially inclusive.

The commitment to change is a significant step towards creating a more equitable and diverse workplace.

Recommendations for Public Sector Policymakers

Addressing the Ethnicity Career Progression Gap in the Public Sector

The public sector bears a significant responsibility in addressing the ethnicity career progression gap, given its statutory obligations under the Equality Act (2010). In light of the inconsistent and often ineffective equity and inclusion approaches currently employed, it is imperative to implement innovative, evidence-based solutions. This includes adopting best practices from both within and outside the public sector, particularly from organisations with proven track records of excellence in specific areas.

Leadership and Expertise

To effectively combat racial discrimination, leaders should engage equity and inclusion experts to design measurable programmes of activity. These initiatives should be comprehensive and tailored to address the specific challenges faced by ethnically diverse employees in career progression.

Human Resources and Long-Term Strategy

The quality of HR in the public sector, and all industries, requires thorough examination. Equity and inclusion experts must collaborate with suitably qualified HR practitioners to ensure effective implementation of diversity initiatives. Furthermore, the professional practice of HR professionals to advise on racial diversity and inclusion should be subject to evaluation.

Rather than viewing equity and inclusion as a temporary issue, organisations should recognise it as a perennial challenge requiring long-term solutions and sustained investment. This approach contrasts with the current over-reliance on short-term fixes through interim consultants and limited project funding.

Performance Management and Accountability

Equity and inclusion performance indicators should be integrated into targets for line managers across all levels and embedded into performance management systems throughout the organisational hierarchy. This ensures accountability and commitment to diversity and inclusion goals at every level of the organisation.

Legislative and Regulatory Measures

Ethnicity Pay Gap and Board Representation

The implementation of ethnicity pay gap legislation should be expedited without further delay. Additionally, the Parker Review committee should incorporate specific targets for Black representation in its recommendations.

External Monitoring and Enforcement

Regulatory bodies should conduct external monitoring of equity and inclusion practices, including measures to address boards lacking racial diversity, as current approaches have proven ineffective.

Organisational Culture and Structural Change

Accountability and Representation

Public sector organisations should be held accountable for the treatment and representation of Black employees, including at board and executive levels. This can be achieved by co-opting expert Black members to provide insights and challenge existing practices.

Addressing Structural Racism

Anti-racism training should be implemented to identify anti-Black racism and Whiteness in organisations. Organisations should strive to reach a level of maturity where structural racism and the role of Whiteness are fully understood as barriers to career progression for ethnically diverse employees. This involves a critical examination of workplace cultures and systems that may inadvertently perpetuate racial inequalities.

By implementing these comprehensive measures, the public sector can lead by example in addressing the ethnicity career progression gap and fostering a more inclusive and equitable work environment for all employees.

Government Recommendations

Modernising Employment Law

Employment law should be updated to address contemporary forms of racism, including:

- Racial microaggressions
- Selective incivilities
- Microsabotage targeting ethnically diverse employees
- Anti-Blackness

These updates would allow HR policies to classify racial microaggressions and selective incivilities as forms of racial harassment and bullying.

Anti-Discrimination Legislation

In addition to proposed mandates for ethnicity pay gap monitoring, organisations should be required to implement comprehensive action plans to address identified disparities. The public sector equality duty should be expanded to include all organisations, thus moving beyond optional diversity, equity, and inclusion (DEI) approaches to ensure consistent and mandatory progress.

Professionalising Equity and Inclusion

- Establish certification for professionals in the equity and inclusion industry
- Develop accreditation for HR professionals in equity and inclusion practices
- Create standardised equity and inclusion accreditation for organisations

Such an accreditation system would help employees and job seekers identify genuinely inclusive organisations and those to avoid!

Career Progression Disparity

Conduct a comprehensive review to address the 'ethnicity career progression gap'.

These recommendations aim to create a more inclusive and equitable work environment by addressing modern forms of racism and transforming organisational culture.

EPILOGUE

As I reflect on my journey and the experiences shared in this book, I am filled with an overwhelming sense of hope and optimism for the future. This book is not just a chronicle of challenges; it is a testament to the resilience, strength and unwavering spirit of Black professionals in the UK workplace.

My deepest wish is that this book will serve as a catalyst for change, empowering Black employees to speak up, use their voices, and advocate for themselves and others. The narratives within these pages are not just accounts of struggle; they are beacons of inspiration, showing that positive change is possible and within our grasp.

While my research has uncovered the challenges faced by Black professionals in the UK, it has also revealed incredible journeys of triumph and progress. We've seen individuals breaking barriers, organisations implementing meaningful changes, and a growing awareness of the importance of equity and inclusion in the workplace.

The path forward is clear, and it's one we'll walk together. By educating ourselves and others about systemic racism, creating inclusive workplace cultures and persistently advocating for change, we're not just dreaming of a more equitable society – we're actively building it.

What fills me with the most hope is the unity and determination I've witnessed. Black professionals are not just persevering; they're thriving, mentoring others and creating supportive communities. This collective strength is transforming challenges into opportunities for growth and positive change.

CONCLUSIONS

This book illuminates the complex interplay between workplace culture and the career progression of Black employees, revealing both challenges and opportunities for positive change. While the research uncovered significant barriers rooted in racialised practices and institutional Whiteness, it also highlights the resilience and potential of Black professionals to excel when given equitable opportunities.

The study brings to light several important discoveries:

Ethnicity Career Progression Gap: Race is the dominant factor that shapes the careers of ethnically diverse employees.

Gendered experiences: Black men and women encounter different forms of discrimination, from overt bias to microaggressions.

Organisational culture: Dominant cultures of Whiteness can create segregated career experiences and two-tier employee systems.

HR and inclusion practices: Current approaches often fall short in addressing racial disparities and promoting genuine inclusion.

Despite these challenges, my research points towards promising avenues for improvement:

Role models: Emphasising the importance of authentic, talented Black role models in leadership positions.

Anti-racism initiatives: Implementing comprehensive anti-racism organisational development approaches.

Talent-management reform: Revising succession-planning and talent-management strategies to ensure equitable opportunities.

HR practice evolution: Transforming HR practices to better support equity and inclusion efforts.

This book serves as a catalyst for change, inviting organisations, leaders and individuals to take meaningful steps towards creating more inclusive and equitable workplaces. By acknowledging the lived experiences of Black employees and implementing targeted solutions, we can work together to bridge the ethnicity career progression gap and unlock the full potential of diverse talent.

The journey towards workplace equality is ongoing, but with concerted effort and a commitment to change, we can create environments where all employees, regardless of race, can thrive and contribute their unique strengths. This research not only sheds light on existing challenges but also paves the way for a more inclusive and prosperous future for all.

Let us embrace this opportunity to transform our workplaces, celebrating diversity and fostering environments where every individual can reach their full potential. Together, we can build a future where career success is determined by talent, dedication and ability, creating a more equitable and vibrant professional landscape for generations to come.

Now that we have reached the end of this journey, I hope the words in this book have inspired you to act and make long-lasting change. I hope you will have learned that racism in the workplace is not just down to a few bad apples and that work is not a bowl of cherries for people of colour. Rather, Black people are rarely able to cherry-pick plum roles in nice environments. Unfortunately, progression of one's career can often go pear-shaped for Black employees. However, when life gives us lemons, we will continue to make lemonade.

As we close this chapter, I invite you to see this not as an ending, but as a beginning. Each of us has the power to be an agent of change, to challenge the status quo, and to create a workplace and a world where everyone can reach their full potential.

The future is bright, and it's one we're creating
together. Let this book be your guide,
your inspiration and your call to action.
Together, we can and will build a more equitable,
inclusive and vibrant society for all.

Dr Marcelle Moncrieffe-Newman

LIST OF ABBREVIATIONS

BAME	A term used to describe people belonging to Black Asian and minority ethnic backgrounds (non-White communities in the UK)
BLM	Black Lives Matter
CGT	Constructivist grounded theory
CRT	Critical race theory
DEI	Diversity, Equity and Inclusion teams or departments within organisations and the related field of expertise
HR	Human Resources
HRM	Human Resource Management

GLOSSARY OF TERMS

Afro-diasporic	A globalised notion of Blackness, global Black community and global Black identity. The term diaspora, as used here, describes the experiences of people who, through slavery, colonialism, imperialism and migration, have been forced to leave their native lands.
Affinity Bias	A form of unconscious bias where individuals tend to favour or warm to those who share similar backgrounds, interests, or experiences as themselves. This can lead to preferential treatment toward colleagues who are perceived as "like us," and inadvertently disadvantage those from different backgrounds, undermining diversity and inclusion practices in the workplace.
Agency	In social science, agency is the capacity of individuals to act independently and to make their own free choices. By contrast, structure is those factors of influence (such as social class, religion, gender, ethnicity, ability, customs, etc.) that determine or limit an agent and his or her decisions.

Anti-Black racism	A pervasive and systemic issue deeply rooted in American and global history, dating back to the colonial era and continuing into the present day. It encompasses a wide range of discriminatory practices, policies and attitudes that specifically target and marginalise people of African descent. Anti-Black racism is not merely the result of individual prejudice but is embedded in societal structures and institutions.
Black ceiling	Complex attitudinal and organisational barriers that constrain Afro-diasporic/ Black and ethnically diverse people from rising to senior leadership.
Co-construction	An approach where researchers collaborate as equal partners throughout the research process.
Constructivist grounded theory (CGT)	A qualitative research methodology developed by Kathy Charmaz that builds upon the original grounded theory approach of Glaser and Strauss. It is primarily used in psychology, education and nursing research to understand social processes and phenomena inductively.
Critical race theory (CRT)	An academic framework and intellectual movement that emerged in the late 1970s and early 1980s, focusing on the intersection of race, law and power in society.

Cultural capital	The skills and knowledge which an individual can draw on to give them an advantage in social life.
Cultural exclusion	Practices that affirm the superiority of one cultural group over others and either excludes those others from full and equal participation or allows inclusion, but only to the degree that the participants give up the practices that are basic to their identity in favour of those of the ruling culture.
Epistemology	The branch of philosophy that studies the nature, origin and limits of human knowledge. It examines fundamental questions about what knowledge is, how it is acquired and how we can justify our beliefs.
Ethnically diverse	Refers to individuals from various cultural, racial and ethnic backgrounds coexisting within a single Western society or region. This diversity encompasses differences in nationality, language, religious beliefs, traditions and cultural practices. This term encompasses all people who are not White.
Halo Effect	A cognitive bias that occurs when an individual's overall impression of a person, often based on a single positive trait or experience, leads to the assumption that this person possesses other, unrelated positive qualities. In the workplace,

	this can result in overlooking areas where the individual may need improvement, potentially affecting decisions on hiring, promotion, and evaluations.
Intersectionality	A theory that considers that the various aspects of humanity, such as class, race, sexual orientation, disability and gender, do not exist separately from each other, but are complexly interwoven and that their relationships are essential to an understanding of the human condition.
Lived experience	Describes, in the context of this research, the first-hand accounts and observations of living as a member of a minority or oppressed group.
Micro-incivility	Subtle behaviours or environmental cues that signal disrespect, exclusion or a lack of belonging to members of marginalised groups or individuals in less powerful positions.
Microaggression	The everyday verbal, non-verbal and environmental slights, snubs or insults, whether intentional or unintentional, that communicate hostile, derogatory or negative messages to target persons based solely upon their marginalised group membership.
Myth of Meritocracy	The belief that success in society or the workplace is solely based on individual

merit, such as hard work, talent, or achievements, rather than on factors like background, identity, bias, or access to opportunities. In practice, structural barriers, social biases, and informal networks often determine advancement.

Nepotism	The practice of favouritism shown to family members or close friends in professional or political settings, often at the expense of more qualified candidates. This form of preferential treatment based on kinship rather than merit has been prevalent throughout history and continues to be a contentious issue in modern workplaces and political spheres.
People of colour	A term primarily used in the United States and Canada to describe any person who is not considered White. This inclusive term encompasses various non-White racial and ethnic groups, including African Americans, Asian Americans, Native Americans, Pacific Islander Americans, multiracial Americans and some Latino Americans.
The Rooney Rule	A policy introduced by the National Football League (NFL) in the USA in 2003 aimed at increasing diversity in leadership positions. The rule requires teams to interview at least two women or persons of colour for prominent positions, and

there's a hiring quota mandating that at least one member of each team's offensive coaching staff must be either ethnically diverse or a woman. The rule has since inspired similar policies in other industries. While the Rooney Rule has faced criticism, it has also been credited with increasing minority representation in NFL leadership roles.

Whiteness	A complex social construct that goes beyond skin colour, encompassing a system of privileges, cultural norms and power structures that benefit those identified as White in Western societies. It refers to the way White people, their customs and culture operate as the default standard against which other groups are compared.
'Woke'	A term that has become increasingly controversial and politicised. For many, being 'woke' means being conscious of various forms of oppression in society and actively seeking to address them. Some critics, particularly on the political right, use 'woke' as a pejorative term to describe what they perceive as excessive political correctness or performative activism. Some conservatives use the term to criticise progressive values and social justice initiatives.

ABOUT THE AUTHOR

Dr Marcelle Moncrieffe-Newman is a distinguished Human Resources Executive and has led corporate functions at board level. Marcelle is a keen advocate for ethical and inclusive values to improve workplace culture. Marcelle received her PhD from Heriot-Watt University, and holds a Master's degree in Human Resource Management and a Bachelor's degree in Law. Marcelle resides in London with her husband and two children.

Areas of Expertise:

- HR
- Race and Equality
- Leadership
- Workplace Culture

To book Dr Marcelle Moncrieffe-Newman for speaking and consultancy engagements, please visit her website:

Website: www.marcellemoncrieffe.com

Instagram: @marcellemoncrieffe

LinkedIn: @Dr Marcelle Moncrieffe

TikTok: @marcy_400

Please share and tag Marcelle in what you or your company is doing to promote racial inclusion via social media or through her website.

APPENDIX

Table 1: Characteristics of Participants

Participant	Gender	Age Range	Ethnicity	Level of Management
1	Female	50–55	Black Caribbean	Middle Manager
2	Female	45–50	Black African	Middle Manager
3	Male	35–40	Black African	Middle Manager
4	Male	45–50	Black Caribbean	Senior Manager
5	Female	45–50	Minority Ethnic	Middle Manager
6	Female	40–45	Black Caribbean	Middle Manager
7	Female	30–35	Black Caribbean	Junior Manager
8	Female	40–45	Minority Ethnic	Senior Manager
9	Female	55–60	Black Caribbean	Middle Manager

10	Male	45–50	Black African	Middle Manager
11	Male	45–50	Black Caribbean	Senior Manager
12	Female	45–50	Black Caribbean	Middle Manager
13	Female	45–50	Black Caribbean	Middle Manager
14	Female	45–50	Black Caribbean	Middle Manager
15	Female	55–60	Black Caribbean	Middle Manager
16	Female	50–55	Black Caribbean	Middle Manager
17	Female	50–55	Black Caribbean	Senior Manager
18	Male	40–45	Black African	Middle Manager
19	Male	50–55	Black Caribbean	Middle Manager
20	Female	55–60	Black Caribbean	Senior Manager
21	Female	50–55	Black African	Middle Manager
22	Female	45–50	Black Caribbean	Middle Manager
23	Female	50–55	Minority Ethnic	Senior Manager

24	Female	50–55	Black Caribbean	Middle Manager
25	Male	45–50	Black Caribbean	Middle Manager
26	Female	45–50	Black African	Senior Manager
27	Female	50–55	Black Caribbean	Senior Manager
28	Male	50–55	Black Caribbean	Senior Manager
29	Female	35–40	Black African	Middle Manager
30	Male	45–50	Black Caribbean	Senior Manager

The author's parents, Theresa and Perry Moncrieffe, on their wedding day in Brent, London, 1971. Both were young and radiated happiness, surrounded by the joyful atmosphere of their celebration.

The author's father, Perry Moncrieffe, during his first year in England at the age of 17 in 1960. He appears youthful and brimming with hope.

Ruby Rosemarie Smart, the author's grandmother, on a day trip to Blackpool, UK, in the 1960s. She looks delighted, standing in front of the coach, eagerly anticipating a wonderful day out.

Members of the Caribbean Social Club in 1981 gather around a prize cake. From left to right: Dorothy Hilton, Theresa Moncrieffe (the author's mother), Alison Hector, and Nelcia Benjamin. There was evident local interest in the work of this vital community group, as their story was featured in the local newspaper.

The Caribbean Social Club's first anniversary dinner in 1981.
Alison Hector, Dorothy Hilton, Peggy Haynes, Nelcia Benjamin,
Patricia Robertson, and Theresa Moncrieffe (the author's mother)
are preparing for a delightful meal.
This event was documented by the local newspaper.

The author with her father, Perry Moncrieffe, at her doctoral graduation ceremony in 2021 in Edinburgh, Scotland. Sadly, Perry passed away while Marcelle was writing the book.

REFERENCES

Abbas, M-S. 2020, The promise of political Blackness? Contesting Blackness, challenging Whiteness and the silencing of racism: A review article, *Ethnicities*, 20(1), 202–222, https://doi.org/10.1177/1468796819834046

ACAS. 2006. Back to basics, in ACAS' Experience of Equality and Diversity in the Workplace. London.

Action for Children. 2024. Blog author Corcoran, K. www.actionforchildren.org.uk/blog/race-and-ethnicity-representation-in-the-media/. Accessed 18 February 2025.

Afzal, N. 2023. *The Race to the Top: How to fight structural racism*. Harper North.

Ajari, J. C. 2024. *Darkening Blackness*. Polity.

Akala. 2018. *Natives: Race & Class in the Ruins of Empire*. Two Roads.

Al-Kaisy, A. 2022. Structural racism in UK newsrooms. Ethical Journalism Network. https://ethicaljournalismnetwork.org/wp-content/uploads/2023/03/EJN_Structural-Racism_April-2023.pdf. Accessed 18 February 2024.

Arday, J. and Mirza, H. S. (eds). 2018. *Dismantling Race in Higher Education: Racism, whiteness and decolonising the academy*. Palgrave Macmillan.

Avery, D. 2011. Why the playing field remains uneven: impediments to promotions in organisations, in: Zedeck, S. (ed.), *APA Handbook of Industrial and Organisational Psychology, Maintaining, Expanding, and Contracting the Organisation*. American Psychological Association, 3, 577–613, https://doi.org/10.1037/12171-016.

Bank of England. 2022. The collection of slavery compensation, 1835–43. www.bankofengland.co.uk/working-paper/2022/the-collection-of-slavery-compensation-1835-43. Accessed 28 December 2024.

Bankole, M. 2024. The Conversation. Kemi Badenoch's views on inequality should worry black Britons. https://theconversation.com/i-research-race-in-politics-kemi-badenochs-views-on-inequality-should-worry-black-britons-244242. Accessed 3 January 2025.

Baroness Casey Review. 2023. Final Report: An independent review into the standards of behaviour and internal culture of the Metropolitan Police Service. www.met.police.uk/SysSiteAssets/media/downloads/met/about-us/baroness-casey-review/update-march-2023/baroness-casey-review-march-2023a.pdf. Accessed 25 November 2024.

Bazelon, C., Vargas, A., Janakiraman. and Olson, M. M. 2023. Quantification of Reparations for Transatlantic Chattel Slavery. The University of the West Indies and The American Society of International Law's Second Symposium on Reparations Under International Law.

BBC News. 2016. Reality Check: Have Leave campaigners changed their Tune? www.bbc.co.uk/news/uk-politics-eu-referendum-36641390. Accessed 30 November 2024.

BBC News. 2020. Edward Enninful: British Vogue editor 'racially profiled' at work. www.bbc.co.uk/news/uk-53425148. Accessed 18 November 2024.

BBC News. 2024a. Commonwealth heads of government to defy UK on slavery reparations. www.bbc.co.uk/news/articles/cd6vy79p750o. Accessed 28 December 2024.

BBC News. 2024b. Slavery reparations: Rachel Reeves rejects calls for UK to act. www.bbc.co.uk/news/articles/cn01ljdl07xo. Accessed 28 December 2024.

BCU. 2022. UK documentaries' damaging portrayals limits Black experience to race, crime and music, new research shows. www.bcu.ac.uk/news-events/news/uk-documentaries-damaging-portrayals-limits-black-experience-to-race-crime-and-music-new-research-shows. Accessed 18 February 2025.

Beckles-Raymond, G. 2020. Implicit Bias, (Global) White Ignorance, and Bad Faith: The Problem of Whiteness and Anti-black racism, *Journal of Applied Philosophy*, 37(2), 169–189, https://doi.org/10.1111/japp.12385.

Ben, J., Kelly, D. and Paradie, Y. 2020. Contemporary anti-racism: A review of effective practice, in: Solomos, J. (ed.), *Routledge International Handbook of Contemporary Racisms*, http://ebookcentral.proquest.com/lib/deakin/detail.action?docID=6121551.

Benson M. and Lewis, C. 2019. Brexit, British People of Colour in the EU-27 and Everyday Racism in Britain and Europe, *Ethnic and Racial Studies*, 42(13), 2211–2228, https://doi.org/10.1080/01419870.2019.1599134.

Bhopal, K. 2018. *White Privilege: The myth of a post-racial society*. Policy Press. http://ebookcentral.proquest.com/lib/hw/detail.action?docID=5349439. Accessed 2 January 2025.

Bhopal, K. 2020. For whose benefit? Black and Minority Ethnic training programmes in higher education institutions in England, *UK British Educational Research Journal*, 46(3) 500–515, DOI: 10.1002/berj.3589.

Black British Voices Project Report. 2023. www.cam.ac.uk/sites/www.cam.ac.uk/files/bbvp_report_pdf_final.pdf. Accessed 18 February 2025.

Black Equity Organisation. 2024. *The State of Black Education in Britain: A Power Analysis for Equity and Change*. https://blackequityorg.com/wp-content/uploads/2024/12/FINAL-THE-STATE-OF-BLACK-EDUCATION-V6.pdf . Accessed 10 March 2025.

Black Presence in Britain. 2010. Black Romans in Britain. https://blackpresence.co.uk/black-romans/. Accessed 3 May 2025.

Blackhistorymonth.org.uk. 2021. Paul Stephenson – The Civil rights pioneer led a victorious boycott against a racist bus company, paving the way for Britain's first race laws. www.blackhistorymonth.org.uk/article/section/civil-rights-movement/paul-stephenson-the-civil-rights-pioneer-led-a-victorious-boycott-against-a-racist-bus-company-paving-the-way-for-britains-first-race-laws/. Accessed 18 February 2025.

Black History Month. 2024. Toxic workplaces: 1 in 3 employees experience microaggressions and discriminatory behaviour. www.blackhistorymonth.org.uk/article/section/news/toxic-workplaces-1-in-3-employees-experience-microaggressions-and-discriminatory-behaviour/. Accessed 18 February 2025.

Brown, M. 2020. Fact check: United Kingdom finished paying off debts to slave-owning families in 2015. USA Today. https://eu.usatoday.com/story/news/factcheck/2020/06/30/fact-check-u-k-paid-off-debts-slave-owning-families-2015/3283908001/. Accessed 28 December 2024.

Burke, P. J. 2018. Trans/forming pedagogical spaces: Race, belonging and recognition in higher education. In: Arday, J. and Mirza, H. S. (eds), *Dismantling Race in Higher Education: Racism, whiteness and decolonising the academy*. Palgrave Macmillan, pp. 365–382.

Busey C. L. and Coleman-King, C. 2020. All Around the World Same Song: Transnational AntiBlack Racism and New (and Old) Directions for Critical Race Theory in Educational Research, *Urban Education*, 1–28. DOI: 10.1177/0042085920927770.

Business in the Community. 2019. The Race at Work Charter: One Year On. www.bitc.org.uk/report/the-race-at-work-charter-one-year-on-2019/. Accessed 2 January 2025.

Business in the Community. 2020. Race at Work: Black Voices Report. www.bitc.org.uk/report/race-at-work-black-voices-report/. Accessed 2 January 2025.

Business in the Community. 2025. Race: Diverse and Inclusive Supply Chains Report. www.bitc.org.uk/race/. Accessed 18 February 2025.

Byrne, B., Alexander, C., Khan, O., Nazroo, J. and Shankley, W. (eds). 2020. *Ethnicity, Race and Inequality in the UK: State of the Nation*. Policy Press.

Charmaz, K. 2000. In: Albrecht, G., Fitzpatrick, S. and Scrimshaw, C. (eds), *The Handbook of Social Studies in Health and Medicine*. Sage.

Chartered Institute of Personnel and Development (CIPD). 2017. Addressing the Barriers to BAME Employee Career Progression to the Top. www.governmentevents.co.uk/wp-content/uploads/2020/10/addressing-the-barriers-to-BAME-employee-career-progression-to-the-top_tcm18-33336.pdf. Accessed 22 November 2024.

Chater, K. 2010. Job Mobility amongst Black People in England and Wales during the Long Eighteenth Century, *Immigrants and Minorities*, 28(2/3), 113–130, https://doi.org/10.1080/02619288.2010.484241.

CIPDHR. 2025. Nearly half of UK adults have experienced workplace discrimination, survey finds. https://learning-news.com/news/ciphr/2025/nearly-half-of-uk-adults-have-experienced-workplace-discrimination-survey-finds. Accessed 18 February 2025.

Commission on Race and Ethnic Disparities. 2021. Report, Cabinet Office. www.gov.uk/government/publications/the-report-of-the-commission-on-race-andethnic-disparities. Accessed 29 December 2024.

Cortina, L. M. 2008. Unseen Injustice: Incivility as Modern Discrimination in Organisations, *The Academy of Management Review*, 33(1), 55–75, doi: 10.5465/amr.2008.27745097.

Cortina, L. M., Kabat-Farr, D., Leskinen, E. A., Huerta, M. and Magley, V. J. 2013. Selective incivility as modern discrimination in organisations: Evidence and impact, *Journal of Management*, 39(6), 1579–1605, https://doi.org/10.1177/0149206311418835

Crenshaw K. 1989. Demarginalising the Intersection of Race and Sex: A Black Feminist Critique of Antidiscrimination Doctrine, Feminist Theory, and Antiracist Politics, University of Chicago Legal Forum, 139–167, https://chicagounbound.uchicago.edu/cgi/viewcontent.cgi?article=1052&context=uclf. Accessed 2 January 2025.

Daniels, S. 2022. *The Anti-Racist Organization: Dismantling Systematic Racism in the Workplace*. Wiley.

Delgado, R. and Stefancic, J. 2017. *Critical Race Theory: An Introduction*. 3rd edition. New York University Press.

Demie, F. and McLean, C. 2017. The Educational Attainment of Black Caribbean Pupils in England, *Journal of Education Policy*, 32(1), 1–18.

Desai, U. 2024. One year on from the Casey Review, here are the reforms still needed to restore trust in the Met. Left Foot

Forward: Leading the UK's progressive debate. https://leftfootforward.org/2024/03/one-year-on-from-the-casey-review-here-are-the-reforms-still-needed-to-restore-trust-in-the-met/. Accessed 28 December 2024.

Dodd, V. and Wilding, M. 2024. UK police risk assessment before riots said far-right threat probably 'minimal'. *The Observer*. Archived from the original on 1 September 2024. www.theguardian.com/uk-news/article/2024/sep/01/uk-police-npcc-risk-assessment-far-right-threat-minimal. Accessed 28 December 2024.

Dow, P. 2024. Report on the Inclusion at Work Panel's recommendations for improving diversity and inclusion practice in the workplace (Sunak Conservative government). www.gov.uk/government/publications/inclusion-at-work-panel-report-on-improving-workplace-diversity-and-inclusion/c281303b-e075-483d-940f-456c92942bec?trk=public_post_comment-text#chairs-cover-letter-to-the-minister-for-women-and-equalities/. Accessed 15 November 2024.

Drydakis, N. 2024. Discrimination and health outcomes in England's black communities amid the cost-of-living crisis: Evaluating the role of inflation and bank rates, *Ethnic and Racial Studies*, 1–29. https://doi.org/10.1080/01419870.2024.2410900.

Eddo-Lodge, R. 2018. *Why I'm no longer talking to White People about race*. Bloomsbury Publishing.

Education Endowment Foundation. 2023. Education Evidence Teaching Learning Toolkit. https://educationendowment

foundation.org.uk/education-evidence/teaching-learning-toolkit. Accessed 3 January 2025.

Ethnicity Facts and Figures. 2023. www.ethnicity-facts-figures.service.gov.uk/education-skills-and-training/after-education/destinations-and-earnings-of-graduates-after-higher-education/latest/#by-ethnicity-average-earnings. Accessed 3 January 2025.

Embrick, G., Domınguez, S. and Karsak, B. 2017. More than Just Insults: Rethinking Sociology's Contribution to Scholarship on Racial Microaggressions, *Sociological Inquiry*, 87(2), 193–206, https://doi.org/10.1111/soin.12184.

Erskine, S. and Bilimoria, D. 2019. White Allyship of Afro-Diasporic Women in the Workplace: A Transformative Strategy for Organisational Change, *Journal of Leadership & Organisational Studies*, 26(3), 319–338, https://doi.org/10.1177/1548051819848993.

Erskine, S. E., Archibold, E. E. and Bilimoria, D. 2021. Afro-Diasporic women navigating the Black ceiling: Individual, relational, and organizational strategies, *ScienceDirect*, https://doi.org/10.1016/j.bushor.2020.10.004 0007-6813.

Fanon, F. 1967. *Black Skin, White Masks*. Grove Press.

Fekete, L. 2020. Reclaiming the fight against racism in the UK, *Institute of Race Relations*, 61(4), 87–95, https://doi.org/10.1177/0306396820911318.

Foster, J., Newburn, T. and Souhami, A. 2005. Assessing the impact of the Stephen Lawrence inquiry, Home Office

Research, Development and Statistics Directorate, www.politieacademie.nl/kennisenonderzoek/kennis/mediatheek/PDF/45875.pdf. Accessed 29 December 2024.

Fox, A. 2023. Child Q: Police strip-search of 15-year-old schoolgirl 'unacceptable behaviour'. *The Independent.* www.independent.co.uk/news/uk/home-news/child-q-police-strip-search-unacceptable-chris-philp-b2412140.html. Accessed 20 November 2024.

Francis, S. 2024. 'Cabinet minister Mark Harper denies Tories have a problem with race'. BBC News.

Fryer P. 1984. *Staying Power: The history of Black people in Britain.* Pluto Press.

Garner, S. J. 2006. The Uses of Whiteness: What sociologists working on Europe can draw from US research on whiteness, *Sociology*, 40(2), 257–275, https://doi.org/10.1177/0038038506062032

Geronimus, A. T. 1992. The weathering hypothesis and the health of African-American women and infants: Evidence and speculations, *Ethnicity & Disease*, 2(3), 207–221, PMID: 1467758.

Gilroy, P. and Gilmore, W. (eds). 2021. *Stuart Hall: Selected Writing on Race and Difference.* Duke University Press.

Greater London Authority. 2024. Ethnicity Pay Gaps in London. www.data.gov.uk/dataset/0b034106-902e-41ad-b4c3-1e0f5a805ffa/ethnicity-pay-gaps-in-london. Accessed 5 January 2025.

Guardian. 2020. UK supermarkets unite after Sainsbury's advert prompts racist backlash. www.theguardian.com/world/2020/nov/28/uk-supermarkets-unite-after-sains-burys- advert-prompts-racist-backlash. Accessed 2 July 2021.

Haynes, K. 2020. Structural inequalities exposed by COVID-19 in the UK: The need for an accounting for care, *Journal of Accounting & Organisational Change*, 16(4), 637–642, https://doi.org/10.1108/JAOC-08-2020-0099.

Hirsch, A. 2018. *Brit(ish)*. Vintage.

House of Commons Library. 2020. Coronavirus: Impact on the labour market, Briefing Paper Number 8898, https://commonslibrary.parliament.uk/research-briefings/cbp-8898/#:~:text=To%20date%2C%20the%20pandemic%20has,to%20have%20become%20economically%20inactive. Accessed 2 January 2024.

House of Commons Library. 2024. Unemployment by ethnic background. Briefing paper no. 6385. https://researchbriefings.files.parliament.uk/documents/SN06385/SN06385.pdf.

Hourston, P. 2023. Cost of living crisis. Institute for Government. www.instituteforgovernment.org.uk/explainer/cost-living-crisis. Accessed 5 January 2025.

Independent, 2020. Coronavirus economic effects hitting ethnic minorities and young people hardest. www.independent.co.uk/news/uk/politics/coronavirus-economic-effect-uk-ethnic-mi-norities-young-people-a9460511.html. Accessed 2 January 2025.

Institute for Public Policy Research & The Difference. 2024. *Racial Disparities in School Exclusions.* www.ippr.org/research/publications/racial-disparities-in-school-exclusions. Accessed 10 March 2025.

Institute of Education. 2024. *Educational Strategies of the Black Middle Classes.* www.ucl.ac.uk/ioe/news/2024/aug/educational-strategies-black-middle-classes. Accessed 10 March 2025.

Jaspal, R., Lopes, B. and Breakwell, G. 2020. British national identity and life satisfaction in ethnic minorities in the United Kingdom, *National Identities*, DOI: 10.1080/14608944.2020.1822793.

Joseph-Salisbury, R., Connelly, L. and Wangari-Jones, P. 2020. The UK is not innocent: Black Lives Matter, policing and abolition in the UK, *Equality, Diversity and Inclusion*, DOI: 10.1108/EDI-06-2020-0170.

Jones, C. 2006. Claudia Jones. Wikipedia. https://en.wikipedia.org/wiki/Claudia_Jones. Accessed 18 February 2025.

Jones, T. 2018. The Ethnic Minority Pay Gap. www.ool.co.uk/blog/the-ethnic-minority-pay-gap/. Accessed 27 November 2024.

Jung, M. and Vargas, J. H. C. 2021. The Black Nonsubject, *Journal of Black Studies*, 52(1), 3–24.

Kellerman, B. 2004. *Bad Leadership*. Harvard Business School Press.

Kendi, I. X. 2019. *How to Be an Antiracist.* One World

Khalili, L. 2017. After Brexit: Reckoning with Britain's Racism and Xenophobia, *Poem*, 5(2–3), 253–265, https://doi.org/10.1080/20519842.2017.1292758.

Kinder, T. 2020. A third of FTSE 100 companies set to miss ethnic diversity targets, *Financial Times*, www.ft.com/content/945ce30e-4762-11ea-aeb3-955839e06441. Accessed 11 November 2024.

King's Speech. 2024. Labour government. https://assets.publishing.service.gov.uk/media/6697f5c10808eaf43b50d18e/The_King_s_Speech_2024_background_briefing_notes.pdfLabour Government. Accessed 3 January 2025.

Komaromi, P. and Singh, K. 2016. Post-referendum racism and xenophobia: The role of social media activism in challenging the normalisation of xeno-racist narratives. Institute of Race Relations. https://irr.org.uk/app/uploads/2016/07/. Accessed 2 January 2025.

Kramer, M. R. 2020. The 10 Commitments Companies Must Make to Advance Racial Justice. *Harvard Business Review*.

Lee, J. 2021. Euro 2020 racist abuse – 11 people arrested. BBC News. www.bbc.co.uk/news/uk-58094408. Accessed 2 January 2025.

Lentin, A. 2018. Beyond denial: 'Not racism' as racist violence, *Journal of Medical and Cultural Studies*, 32, 400–414, https://doi.org/10.1080/10304312.2018.1480309

Lammy Review, Final Report. 2017. GOV. UK. www.gov.uk/government/publications/lammy-review-final-report. Accessed 2 January 2025.

Li, Y. and Heath, A. 2020. Persisting disadvantages: A study of labour market dynamics of ethnic unemployment and earnings in the UK (2009–2015), *Journal of Ethnic and Migration Studies*, 46(5), 857–878, DOI: 10.1080/1369183X.2018.1539241.

Lillis, T. 2003. Student writing as 'academic literacies': Drawing on Bakhtin to move from critique to design, *Language and Education*, 17(5), 192–207.

London Assembly Report. 2024. The Casey Review: One Year On. https://gla.moderngov.co.uk/documents/s109946/06%20Casey%20one%20year%20on%20report%2020240306.pdf. Accessed 15 November 2024.

Macpherson, W. 1999. The Stephen Lawrence Inquiry: Report of an inquiry. TSO.

Mahoney, M. 1997. Racial Construction and Women as Differentiated Actors. In: Delgado, R. and Stefancic, J. 2017. *Critical Race Theory: An Introduction*. 3rd edition. New York University Press, pp. 305–309.

Manderson, M. 2022. *From Hood to Headship: A Black Woman's Journey to Becoming a Headteacher*. Peaches Publications.

McCluney, C., Robotham, K., Lee, S., Smith, R. and Durkee, M. 2019. The Costs of Code-Switching. *Harvard Business Review*. https://hbr.org/2019/11/the-costs-of-codeswitching. Accessed 19 November 2024.

McCluney, C. L., Bryant, C. M., King, D. D. and Ali, A. A. 2017. Calling in Black: A dynamic model of racially traumatic events, resourcing, and safety, *Equality, Diversity and Inclusion*, 36(8), 767–786, https://doi.org/10.1108/EDI-01-2017-0012.

McCluney C. L., King D. D., Bryant C. M. and Ali A. A. 2020. From 'Calling in Black' to 'Calling for Antiracism Resources': The need for systemic resources to address systemic racism, *Equality, Diversity and Inclusion*, DOI: 10.1108/EDI-07-2020-0180.

McGregor-Smith, R. 2017. Race in the Workplace report: The McGregor-Smith Review, Department for Business, Energy & Industrial Strategy. https://assets.publishing.service.gov.uk/government/uploads/system/uploads/attachment_data. Accessed 1 November 2024.

Meer, N. 2018. Race Equality after Enoch Powell, *The Political Quarterly*, 89(3), DOI: 10.1111/1467-923X.12546.

Miller, P. 2020a. Race Discrimination, the Politics of Knowledge, and Cultural Inequality in England. In: Papa, R., (ed.), *Handbook on Promoting Social Justice in Education*. Springer Nature. https://doi.org/10.1007/978-3-030-14625-2_43.

Miller, P. 2020b. Anti-racist school leadership: making 'race' count in leadership preparation and development. *Professional Development in Education*. Routledge/Taylor & Francis.

Millington, G. 2011. 'Race', Culture and the Right to the City. www.palgraveconnect.com/pc/doifinder/10.1057/9780230353862.0001. Accessed 29 December 2024.

Mirror. 2024. Middlesbrough rioters stop traffic to check if drivers are 'white' in shocking footage. www.mirror.co.uk/news/uk-news/middlesbrough-rioters-stop-traffic-check-33393888. Accessed 28 December 2024.

Mohdin, A. and Walker, P. 2021. Bodies credited in UK Race Review distance themselves from findings, *The Guardian*. www.theguardian.com/world/2021/apr/12/bodies-credited-inuk-race-review-distance-themselves-from-findings. Accessed 2 November 2024.

Moncrieffe, M. 2021. What impact does the workplace culture of public sector institutions have on the career progression of Black employees? Doctor of Business Administration Thesis. Heriot-Watt University.

Morrison, T. 1993. *Playing in the Dark: Whiteness and the Literary Imagination*. Vintage.

Mungin, R. and Stock, E. 2020. Corporate allyship: Show your work or quiet down. CIO. www.cio.com/article/3567511/corporate-allyship-show-your-work-or-quiet-down.html. Accessed 16 March 2025.

Monrose, K. 2023. Black British Voices: The findings. www.cam.ac.uk/stories/black-british-voices-report. Accessed 18 February 2025.

Narayan, J. 2019. British Black Power: The anti-imperialism of political Blackness and the problem of nativist socialism, *The Sociological Review*, 67(5), 945–967, https://doi.org/10.1177/0038026119845550.

Ndiaye, N. 2024. Scripts of Blackness: Early Modern Performance Culture and the Making of Race, *French Studies*, 78(1), 151–152.

Office for Equality and Opportunity. 2023. Positive Action in the Workplace. Government Publications. www.gov.uk/government/publications/positive-action-in-the-workplace-guidance-for-employers/positive-action-in-the-workplace#executive-summary. Accessed 3 January 2025.

Office for National Statistics. 2020. Effects of Taxes and Benefits on UK Household Income: Financial Year Ending 2019. www.ons.gov.uk/peoplepopulationandcommunity/personalandhouseholdfinances/incomeandwealth/bulletins/theeffectsoftaxesandbenefitsonhouseholdincome/previousReleases. Accessed 30 December 2024.

Ossenkop, C., Vinkenburg, C., Jansen, P. and Ghorashi, H. 2015. Ethnic diversity and social capital in upward mobility systems: Problematising the permeability of intra-organisational career boundaries, *Career Development International*, 20(5), 539–558, https://doi.org/10.1108/CDI-12-2013-0148.

Oteka, C. 2022. Black in Fact – Beyond the White Gaze: The examination of black representation in documentaries for UK audiences. Birmingham City University. https://bcuassets.blob.core.windows.net/docs/black-in-fact-csu2022011-lhc-report--otekav4lowres4222-132887820328770199.pdf. Accessed 28 December 2024.

Ozturk, M. B. and Berber, A. 2020. Racialised professionals' experiences of selective incivility in organisations: A multi-level analysis of subtle racism, *UK Human Relations*, 1–27, DOI: 10.1177/0018726720957727.

Parker, J. 2016. A Report into the Ethnic Diversity of UK Boards: Beyond One by '21', The Parker Review Committee. www.gov.uk/government/publications/ethnic-diversity-of-uk-boards-the-parker-review. Accessed 2 January 2025.

Parker, J. 2020. Ethnic Diversity Enriching Business Leadership: An update report from The Parker Review, EY. https://assets.ey.com/content/dam/ey-sites/ey-com/en_uk/news/2020/02/ey-parker-review-2020-report-final.pdf. Accessed 2 January 2025.

Parker Review Report. 2024. https://parkerreview.co.uk/wp-content/uploads/2024/03/The-Parker-Review-March-2024.pdf. Accessed 28 November 2024.

Parks-Yancy, R. 2006. The effects of social group membership and social capital resources on careers, *Journal of Black Studies*, 36(4), 515–545, DOI: 10.1177/0021934704273501.

Parveen, N. 2021. Priti Patel describes Black Lives Matter Protests as 'Dreadful', *The Guardian*, www.theguardian.com/politics/2021/feb/12/priti-patel-hits-out-at-dreadful-Black-lives-matters-protests. Accessed 2 July 2021.

Paynter, R. 2001. The Cult of Whiteness in Western New England. In: Orser, C. (ed.) *Race and the Archaeology of Identity*. University of Utah Press, pp. 125–142.

Peach, C. 1998. South Asian and Caribbean ethnic minority housing choice in Britain, *Urban Studies*, 35(10), 1657–1680, https://doi.org/10.1080/01419870802604024.

Platt, L. and Nandi, A. 2020. Ethnic diversity in the UK: New opportunities and changing constraints, *Journal of Ethnic and Migration Studies*, 46(5), 839–856, DOI: 10.1080/1369183X.2018.1539229.

Police Foundation. 2023. The Met must reinvent itself or die. www.police-foundation.org.uk/2023/03/casey-review-the-met-must-reinvent-itself-or-die/. Accessed 24 November 2024.

Public Health England. 2020. Disparities in the risk and outcomes of COVID-19. https://assets.publishing.service. Accessed 2 January 2025.

Ray, V. 2019. A Theory of Racialised Organisations, *American Sociological Review*, 84(1), 26–53, https://doi.org/10.1177/0003122418822335.

Reddie, A. G. 2020. Racial Justice for the Windrush Generation in Great Britain, *The Ecumenical Review*, World Council of Churches.

Reuters. 2021. Race and leadership in the news media 2021: Evidence from five markets.

Rhimes, S. 2015. *The Year of Yes: How to Dance It Out, Stand in the Sun and Be Your Own Person*. Simon & Schuster.

Roediger, D. 1999. *Black on White: Black Writers on What it Means to be White*. Schocken.

Romani, L., Holck, L. and Risberg, A. 2019. Benevolent discrimination: Explaining how human resources professionals can be blind to the harm of diversity initiatives, *Organisation*, 26(3), 371–390, https://doi.org/10.1177/1350508418812585.

Ross, K. M. 2020. Call it what it is: Anti-Blackness. www.nytimes.com/2020/06/04/opinion/georgefloyd-anti-Blackness.html. Accessed 2 January 2025.

Royal College of General Practitioners. 2021. RCGP Response to Commission on Race and Ethnic Disparities report. www.rcgp.org.uk/about-us/news/2021/april/rcgp-response-to-commission-on-race-and-ethnic-disparities-report.aspx. Accessed 29 December 2024.

Runnymede Trust. 2017. Intersecting inequalities: The impact of austerity on Black and Minority Ethnic women in the UK. www.intersecting-inequalities.com/projects. Accessed 2 January 2025.

Runnymede Trust. 2022. Falling Faster amidst a Cost-of-Living Crisis: Poverty, Inequality and Ethnicity in the UK. http://cdn.prod.website-files.com/61488f992b58e687f1108c7c/633d8007a3bfa49bd4cd0fa8_Runnymede%20Briefing%20Cost%20of%20Living%20FINAL.pdf. Accessed 20 November 2024.

Rush, A. 2007. Reshaping British History: The Historiography of West Indians in Britain in the Twentieth Century, *History Compass*, 5, 463–484, DOI: 10.1111/j.1478-0542.2007.00403.x.

Sandoiu, A. 2021. 'Weathering': What are the health effects of stress and discrimination? www.medicalnewstoday.com/articles/weathering-what-are-the-health-effects-of-stress-and-discrimination#An-apt-and-troubling-metaphor. Accessed 22 November 2024.

Sensoy, O. and DiAngelo, R. 2017. 'We are All for Diversity, but …': How Faculty Hiring Committees Reproduce Whiteness and Practical Suggestions for How They Can Change, *Harvard Educational Review*, 8(4), https://doi.org/10.17763/1943-5045-87.4.557.

Seifert, R. and Wang, W. 2018. Race discrimination at work: The moderating role of trade unionism in English local government, *Industrial Relations Journal*, 49(3), 259–277, https://doi.org/10.1111/irj.12214.

Sivanandan, A. 1982. *A Different Hunger*. Pluto Press.

Sky Sports. 2024. Reidy, C. An insight into Black managers in English football. www.skysports.com/football/news/11096/13229632/black-history-month-against-the-odds-an-insight-into-black-managers-in-english-football. Accessed 3 May 2025.

Smith, W. A., Allen, W. R. and Danley, L. L. 2007. 'Assume the position … you fit the description': Psychosocial experiences and racial battle fatigue among African American male college students, *American Behavioural Scientist*, 51(4), 551–578, https://doi.org/10.1177/0002764207307742.

Stopforth, S., Kapadia, D., Nazroo, J. and Bécares, L. 2022. The enduring effects of racism on health: Understanding direct and indirect effects over time, *SSM - Population Health*, DOI:10.1016/j.ssmph.2022.101217.

The Week. 2023. Reparations from the UK? https://theweek.com/royal-family/1023334/pros-and-cons-of-british-colonial-reparations. Accessed 28 November 2024.

Thompson, F. 2023. *Metropolitan Police: What are the key findings of the Casey review? The Independent.* www.independent.co.uk/news/uk/louise-casey-metropolitan-police-mark-rowley-lgbtq-asian-b2304863.html. Accessed 1 November 2024.

University of Leeds, 2022. Cost of living crisis highlights racial inequalities. https://essl.leeds.ac.uk/sociology/news/article/1623/cost-of-living-crisis-highlights-racial-inequalities. Accessed 28 November 2024.

Uwagba, O. 2020. *Whites on Race and Other Falsehoods.* Harper Collins

Versi, M. 2016. Brexit has given voice to racism – and too many are complicit. *The Guardian.* www.theguardian.com/commentisfree/2016/jun/27/brexit-racism-eu-referendum-racist-incidents-politicians-media. Accessed 3 May 2025.

Virdee, S. and McGeever, B. 2018. Racism, Crisis, Brexit. *Ethnic and Racial Studies*, 41(10), 1802–1819, https://eprints.bbk.ac.uk/id/eprint/20173/1/Racism%20Crisis%20Brexit.pdf.

Visibility Project. 2014. On Moya Bailey, Misogynoir, and why both are important. www.thevisibilityproject.com/2014/05/27/on-moya-bailey-misogynoir-and-why-both-are-important/. Accessed 3 January 2025.

Wallace, D. and Joseph-Salisbury, R. 2022. Blackness and the Politics of Schooling, *Journal of Education Policy*, 37(4), 531–546.

Wang, W. and Seifert, R. 2020. BAME Staff and Public Service Motivation: The Mediating Role of Perceived Fairness in English Local Government, *Journal of Business Ethics*, 161, 653– 664, DOI: 10.1007/s10551-018-3953-8.

Watch This Space. 2024. The value of diversity and inclusion in the workplace in stats. www.watchthisspace.uk/diversity-inclusion-stats/. Accessed 18 February 2025.

Webber, F. and Edmond-Pettitt, A. 2018. The embedding of state hostility: A background paper on the Windrush Scandal, Institute of Race Relations, Briefing Paper no. 11. https://irr.org.uk/product/the-embedding-of-state-hostility-a-background-paper-on-the-windrush-scandal/. Accessed 2 January 2025.

West, K. 2025. *The Science of Racism: Everything you need to know but probably don't – yet*. Pan Macmillan.

White, N. 2022. Black and Asian unemployment rate more than double that of white people as recession looms. *The Independent*. www.independent.co.uk/news/uk/home-news/jobs-black-asian-unemployment-rate-statistics-b2072994.html. Accessed 25 November 2024.

Williams, R. 2015. African London. Black History Month Article. www.Blackhistorymonth.org.uk/article/section/real-stories/african-london/. Accessed 2 January 2025.

Wyatt, M. and Silvester, J. 2015. Reflections on the labyrinth: Investigating Black and minority ethnic leaders' career experiences, *Human Relations*, 68(8), 1243–1269, https://doi.org/10.1177/0018726714550890.

Yuval-Davis, N. 1999. Institutional racism, cultural diversity and citizenship: Some reflections on reading the Stephen Lawrence Inquiry Report, *Sociological Research Online*, 4(1), https://doi.org/10.5153/sro.235.

USEFUL LINKS AND FURTHER READING

ACAS. Preventing race discrimination – Race discrimination – www.acas.org.uk/race-discrimination/preventing-race-discrimination

Afzal, N. 2023. *The Race to the Top: How to fight structural racism.* Harper North.

Black British Voices Project Report, 2023. www.cam.ac.uk/sites/www.cam.ac.uk/files/bbvp_report_pdf_final.pdf.

Daniels, S. 2022. *The Anti-Racist Organization: Dismantling Systematic Racism in the Workplace.* Wiley.

Eddo-Lodge R. 2018. *Why I'm no longer talking to White People about race.* Bloomsbury Publishing.

Podcast Episode 122: Inequality, Social Justice & HR: Dr Marcelle Moncrieffe, Former Chief People Officer, City of London Corporation – From Babies with Love

Podcast Episode 20: Dr Marcelle Moncrieffe FCIPD – Group Chief People Culture and Communications Officer – Oakleaf

Moncrieffe, M. 2021. What impact does the workplace culture of public sector institutions have on the career progression of Black employees? Doctor of Business Administration Thesis. Heriot-Watt University. MoncrieffeM_1021_ebsSS.pdf

One Step Forward, Two Steps Black Podcast https://www.marcellemoncrieffe.com/

Roberts, Sarah Jakes. 2024. *Power Moves: Invite Your Confidence and Become a Force.* W Publishing Group.

St Fleur, D. 2021. *Deeper than Work: How Women of Color can make more money, have more impact and thrive in the corporate world.* Amazon.

Ross K. M. 2020. Call it what it is: Anti-Blackness, www.nytimes.com/2020/06/04/opinion/georgefloyd-anti-Blackness.html.

West, K. 2025. *The Science of Racism: Everything you need to know but probably don't – yet.* Pan Macmillan

Workplace Inclusion Consultancy
https://includableconsultancy.com/

INDEX

STUDY NOTES

Study Notes

Study Notes

Study Notes

Study Notes

Study Notes

Printed in Dunstable, United Kingdom

76943412R00178